California

by Richard Minnich

Richard Minnich comes from a long line of
serious travelers. Bitten by the travel bug at an
early age, he is fortunate to have seen a good bit
of the world. To him, writing about his travels is
fulfilling and a welcome diversion to his life as a
writer/producer of theater and film. Essential
California is his first guidebook. Originally from
Pennsylvania, he currently resides in
Los Angeles.

Above: *Mural at Venice Beach*

AA Publishing

Frog Jumping Jubilee, Angel's Camp

Written by Richard Minnich
Updated by Julie Jares

Reprinted Nov 1998; Reprinted Apr 1999
Reprinted May 2001
Reprinted 2004. Information verified and updated.
Reprinted Aug 2004
Reprinted 2006. Information updated and verified.

© Automobile Association Developments Limited 2006

Published by AA Publishing, a trading name of Automobile Association Developments Limited, whose registered office is Fanum House, Basing View, Basingstoke, Hampshire RG21 4EA. Registered number 1878835.

Find out more about AA Publishing and the wide range of travel publications and services the AA provides by visiting our website at www.theAA.co.uk /bookshop.

A02352
Atlas section and cover maps
© MAIRDUMONT/ Falk Verlag 2005

Colour separation: Keenes, Andover
Printed and bound in Italy by Printers Trento srl

Contents

About this Book

This book is divided into five sections to cover the most important aspects of your visit to California.

Viewing California pages 5–14
An introduction to California by the author
    California's Features
    Essence of California
    The Shaping of California
    Peace and Quiet
    California's Famous

Top Ten pages 15–26
The author's choice of the Top Ten places to see in California, each with practical information.

What to See pages 27–90
The four main areas of California, each with its own brief introduction and an alphabetical listing of the main attractions.
    Practical information
    Snippets of "Did You Know…" information
    4 suggested walks
    4 suggested tours
    2 features

Where To… pages 91–116
Detailed listings of the best places to eat, stay, shop, take the children and be entertained.

Practical Matters pages 117–24
A highly visual section containing essential travel information.

Maps
All map references are to the individual maps found in the What to See section of this guide.
For example, Alcatraz has the reference ✚ 29D6—indicating the page on which the map is located and the grid square in which the island is to be found. A list of the maps that have been used in this travel guide can be found in the index.

Prices
Where appropriate, an indication of the cost of an establishment is given by **$** signs:
$$$** denotes higher prices, **$$** denotes average prices, while **$ denotes lower charges.

Star Ratings
Most of the places described in this book have been given a separate rating:
✪✪✪   Do not miss
✪✪   Highly recommended
✪   Worth seeing

Viewing
California

Above: *Sculpture on Rodeo Drive,
Los Angeles*

Richard Minnich's California

Describing California and its people is like trying to describe a beautiful painting: most people will have a different perspective and feeling. The word that most readily comes to mind is *extreme*. Nowhere on earth can one find such extreme variances of scenic splendor or inhabitants. Within an 80-mile (129km) span are the highest and lowest elevations in the United States, each with its own unique beauty.

From the very first person to set foot in the state to its most recent émigré, the trait that has most greatly characterized the state's populace is a deep commitment to adventure. California seems to define the concept of diversity with both its geography and inhabitants. With nearly every culture represented throughout the state, there are enough dining and entertainment selections to suit everyone's desire.

California offers virtually every type of terrain, from desert to ocean to mountain, and environments ranging from small farming communities to giant metropolises that teem with cultural activity 24 hours a day.

If you're simply looking for rest and recuperation on your vacation, this is the place to visit. California is the epitome of "laid back," even in its busiest cities. At the same time the state is the nation's leader for fashion and fun.

So often when traveling, one's preconceived notion of a destination and the reality of that destination vary greatly. But whatever your most romantic visions of California might be, rest assured your visit to this kaleidoscopic state will not disappoint. It is almost impossible to overestimate the grandeur that awaits.

The Living Desert, a 1,200-acre (486-ha) garden and wild animal park in Palm Desert

California's Features

Geography
- Population: 35,500,000.
- Land area: 155,959sq miles (399,894sq km).
- Highest point: Mount Whitney (14,494ft/4,419m).
- Lowest point: Death Valley (282ft/86m below sea level).
- Capital: Sacramento.

Economic Factors
- California is the leading agricultural economy in the US, primarily because of its fruit crops: prunes, oranges, grapes, peaches, apricots, figs, lemons, avocados, dates, nectarines and rice plums. Other agriculture products include cotton, walnuts, almonds, sugar beet, tomatoes, eggs, turkeys, sunflowers and honey.
- Napa and Sonoma valleys (► 88) are famous for their wineries. Southern California has both film and television production and manufactures military aircraft and missiles.

Sports and Leisure
- Almost every conceivable sport, from boating and other watersports to sky-diving and rollerblading.

Animal Life
- The Pacific Ocean is home to humpback whales, sea otters, seals, sea lions, dolphins, elephant seals, and blue whales, the largest mammals in the world, as well as hundreds of species of smaller fish.

The pupfish (desert sardine) has even managed to survive in arid Death Valley (► 71).
- Land animals include bison, deer, Roosevelt elk, mountain goats, big-horn sheep, mountain lions, bobcats, wild burros and black bear.
- Desert creatures include iguanas, chuckawallas, pronghorn antelope, coyotes, kangaroo rats and various insects and reptiles, including the dangerous black widow spider and the poisonous rattlesnake.
- Birdlife ranges from the exotic white-faced ibis and the tiny hummingbird to the bald and golden eagle and the mundane sea gull.

Plants
- Unique trees in California are the eucalyptus, sequoias, redwoods, Joshua trees and many varieties of palm. Various cacti and flowers also abound year-round.

Climate
California is known for its diversity of climates. Generally speaking, the south is warmer and the north cooler. The bay areas are renowned for their fog. The mountainous areas are known for pleasant summers and snowy winters at the higher elevations. The San Joaquin and Sacramento valleys are extremely hot during the summer months and cool and foggy the rest of the year. As a rule, most parts of the state are cool in the evenings.

USC Trojans in the Coliseum

7

Essence of California

One of the best things about California is that you rarely have to plan your vacation around the seasons. If you wish to relax on the beach, accommodations range from luxurious oceanside resorts to basic camping facilities. If you want continuous entertainment, the state abounds with theme parks, fairs and festivals.

For the explorer or seeker of beauty, the natural habitat is varied and unbeatable. For a tour of the coastline, the Amtrak rail system runs from the top to the bottom of the state and features plush, picture-windowed lounge cars. The landscape is great for the photographer.

Bottom: *Zabriskie Point, Death Valley National Monument*

THE 10 ESSENTIALS

If you only have a short time to visit California, or would like to get a really complete picture of the state, here are the essentials:

• **Take a drive (or train)** along California's famous Route 1 for fantastic ocean views to the west and spectacular rolling hills or majestic mountain ranges to the east.

• **Spend the day** at one of the many beaches. Surf, sun or rent a bicycle, boogieboard or rollerblades.

• **Walk across the Golden Gate Bridge** (➤ 19) from San Francisco to Marin County. Spend an hour or so wandering around the small towns on the other side, then you can either walk or hop on a ferry back to San Francisco. Finish the day with a cable-car ride to view the city's marvellous architecture.

• **Spend a day hiking or backpacking** in one of the many national or state parks. The Joshua Tree National Monument is an especially good one (➤ 73).

• **Experience the excitement** of professional sports in San Francisco, San Diego or Los Angeles or attend a horse race at one of the major tracks.

• **Go window-shopping** along Beverly Hill's exclusive Rodeo Drive (➤ 48, 49) or El Paseo Drive in Palm Springs (➤ 107).

• **Take a drive through the Napa Valley** wine country, stopping at any of the wineries for a tour and some wine-tasting (➤ 88). This is also an excellent place to buy your souvenirs to take back home.

• **Visit a theme park.** Disneyland is the most well-known (➤ 18), but Balboa Park/San Diego Zoo is exciting too (➤ 16).

• **Take the one-day cruise** from San Pedro or Newport Beach across to Catalina Island (➤ 17).

• **Tour one of Hollywood's** motion picture studios for an inside look at the making of screen magic. Universal Studios (➤ 54) is the most famous.

Above: *Universal Studios*
Below: *Characters from Sea World, San Diego*

9

The Shaping of California

c7,000BC
La Brea Tar Pit woman, first known LA resident, dies mysteriously.

AD1542
Juan Cabrillo enters "the Bay of Smokes" (San Pedro Bay).

1579
Sir Francis Drake claims San Francisco Bay area for Queen Elizabeth I.

1769
Franciscan monk Junípero Serra founds Mission San Diego de Alcala.

1777
Monterey becomes capital of Spanish-controlled California.

1781
Pueblo de Los Angeles is founded by 44 settlers of European, African and Native American heritages.

1790
Los Angeles population reaches 139.

1821
Spain grants independence to California.

1846
President Polk tries to purchase California (including parts of the present-day New Mexico) from Mexico for $40 million. Mexican-American War begins; US flag raised in San Francisco and Los Angeles.

1847
Yerba Buena, whose population is just a few hundred, is renamed San Francisco.

1848
James Wilson Marshall discovers gold at Coloma.

1849
Gold Rush attracts over 300,000 prospectors. San Jose becomes state capital.

1850
California joins the US as its 31st state.

1853
Levi Strauss creates denim jeans in San Francisco; Don Matteo Keller plants the state's first orange trees.

1854
Sacramento becomes the state capital.

1857
Fort Tejon earthquake (8.0) rocks Los Angeles.

1858
Wine industry is born.

1862
Telegraph connects San Francisco and New York.

1869
Railroad joins the east and west coasts.

1873
First cable-car in San Francisco. University of California established at Berkeley.

1881
First *Los Angeles Times* rolls off the presses. First snowfall in downtown LA.

The San Francisco earthquake of 1906

1882
First LA telephone directory is a mere three pages long.

1906
Earthquake and fire levels most of San Francisco.

1907
George Feeth introduces surfing to Southern California.

1908
Colonel William Selig opens first Hollywood film studio to produce *In the Sultan's Power*.

1915
Telephone connects New York and San Francisco.

1927
Charles Lindbergh's *The Spirit of St. Louis* is built by Ryan Airlines in San Diego.

1929
First Academy Awards presentation at the Hollywood Roosevelt Hotel.

1933
Donald Douglas builds first mass-produced commercial aircraft, the DC-2, at Santa Monica.

1935
Statewide irrigation system turns the arid central valley plains into a lush green oasis.

1936
San Francisco-Oakland Bay Bridge opens.

1937
Golden Gate Bridge opens.

1940
First western freeway, Arroyo Seco Parkway, opens in LA.

1942
Japanese shell Santa Barbara.

1945
United Nations signs charter in San Francisco.

1947
Anti-Communist hearings lead to Hollywood black-listing.

Marilyn Monroe

1955
Disneyland opens.

1962
California becomes the most populous state in America.

1963
Marilyn Monroe dies.

1964
Beatles play Hollywood Bowl.

1968
Senator Robert Kennedy assassinated at LA's Ambassador Hotel.

1977
Silicon Valley develops Apple II, first market-able personal computer.

1980
Ronald Reagan, actor and ex-California Governor becomes US president.

1984
California hosts Summer Olympics.

1989
Earthquake (7.1) shakes San Francisco.

1992
Worst rioting in American history in Los Angeles after verdict in the police-beating trial of Rodney King.

1995
Jury acquits O. J. Simpson for the murders of Nicole Brown Simpson and Ronald Goldman.

1998–2000
California celebrates 150 years since the discovery of gold, the gold rush and the state's creation.

2003
Actor Arnold Schwarzenegger becomes California's 38th governor in a controversial recall election.

Peace & Quiet

Rarely can you visit an area and have so many options to choose from to amuse and entertain yourself, but in California there are also as many choices that offer nothing but relaxation and reflection in tranquil surroundings.

Southern California

Separate from the mainland, the picturesque Channel Islands National Park and Catalina Island (► 17) provide a respite from the hustle and bustle of the city. Biking and horseback riding are offered on the islands, and both are wonderful for hiking.

Back on the mainland, in Santa Monica Mountains National Recreation Area hiking trails abound, and the coastline views are incredible from Sandstone Peak, its highest elevation at 3,111ft (948m). Nearby Point Dume is a popular secluded beach great for winter-time whale-watching. For nature at its best, visit the undeveloped Crystal Cove State Park near Laguna Beach and Torrey Pines State Reserve near La Jolla, in San Diego.

If you enjoy the desert, Anza-Borrego Desert State Park (► 82) and Lost Palm Oasis in Joshua Tree National Monument (► 73) provide incredible hiking and camping. As the ocean calms with its cascading sound and magnetic emanations, the desert soothes with unremitting sun and vast stillness. The extreme heat and dryness attract numerous birds, mammals and reptiles as well as intriguing plant life. Campgrounds are scattered throughout, many amid great climbing rocks, if you tire of merely sitting.

Rock-climbers are often seen scaling the smooth granite boulders at Joshua Tree National Monument

Central California

Gaviota State Park, Refugio State Beach and El Capitan State Beach, all in Santa Barbara County, offer perfect alternatives to the more crowded outdoor areas. After some quiet time on the beach, explore the hills and hiking trails just a short distance away.

Near Carmel, the Point Lobos State Reserve offers spectacular views of the Monterey cypress. Relax in the sun or take a more strenuous 50-mile (81-km) bicycle ride through the Carmel Valley.

Northern California

If you like to hike, head for the Lost Coast Trail in Humboldt County. Just south of Eureka, the King Range National Conservation Area is a favorite with back-packers. Coastal redwoods and Roosevelt elk can be seen in abundance in the Prairie Creek Redwoods State Park. In the Shasta area, the Trinity Alps Wilderness offers great trails, or if you'd rather ride, there are exotic llamas for hire. In the Sierra Nevadas, the best hiking is in the aptly named Desolation Wilderness near Lake Tahoe (► 75).

Rock-climbers swear that scaling the granite face of such towering spires as El Capitan and Half Dome, in Yosemite National Park (► 26), is both invigorating and relaxing at the same time.

Gardens

If you don't want to leave the metropolitan areas, you can still escape by visiting one of the many botanical gardens in the state. The Self-Realization Centers in both Los Angeles and San Diego provide peaceful gardens in which to meditate. One little-known area is the Greystone estate (now a park) just off Doheny Drive, above Sunset in Los Angeles. The Asian temples of the major cities are also quiet spots, and many are surrounded by beautiful Zen gardens.

Stowe Lake, Golden Gate National Park

The Beach

Take some time out to experience the beach side of the Golden State. Nap on one of the many strands, or better yet, spend a night or two at a beachside hotel. Let the roar of the Pacific Ocean drown out civilization's daily annoyances and the sun recharge your solar batteries. Add to this the gentle sea breezes through your hair, and the refreshing feel of salt water on your body.

13

California's Famous

Film and Television

Hollywood has created hundreds of celebrities, from Marilyn Monroe to John Wayne. Directors Francis Ford Coppola and George Lucas, of *American Graffiti* and *Star Wars* fame respectively, are both Northern Californians who have set a standard for excellence in the film industry.

Music

Jerry Garcia, leader of the Grateful Dead, inspired the San Francisco music scene of the 1960s, which rocketed such musicians as Janis Joplin and The Jefferson Airplane to stardom. Jim Morrison, poet and singer for the Doors, was a student at UCLA film school and is considered one of the great musicians to emerge from Southern California. And you can't mention California music without including the Beach Boys, who captured Southern California's surf lifestyle with their music.

One of Hollywood's most famous sons: John Wayne

Literature

Dashiell Hammett, author of *The Maltese Falcon*, was a native Californian, and Beat Generation hero Jack Kerouac claimed San Francisco as his adult home (➤ 38). Jack London hails from Glen Ellen in Sonoma Valley (➤ 88), and John Steinbeck was born in Salinas (➤ 85).

Explorers

John Muir, founder of the Sierra Club, considered California paradise, and 1856 presidential candidate John C. Fremont understandably preferred exploring California to politics. Who wouldn't?

Politics

Two 20th-century US presidents emerged from the state: Richard Nixon and Ronald Reagan. Nixon is remembered for his scandal-caused resignation and Reagan was the first actor elected to the highest office in the nation.

Business

Media mogul William Randolph Hearst (➤ 20), E. W. Scripps, founder of United Press International, and Orville Redenbacher, the popcorn king, all hail from the state.

Scandal
Author/humorists Artemus Ward, Bret Harte, Mark Twain, Ambrose Bierce and Joaquin Miller hung out together in 1860s San Francisco. Their friend, Adah Menken, scandalized the city by appearing in Byron's *Mazeppa* wearing nothing but a flesh-colored body suit. She was strapped backwards on a horse as it galloped up a three-story stage mountain complete with waterfalls and chasms.

Top Ten

Above: *Parking on Rodeo Drive*

1
Balboa Park

Balboa Park, the pride of San Diego

This immense expanse of parks and museums includes the world-renowned San Diego Zoo.

A 100-tone chime serenades from the 200-ft (61-m) California Tower, creating an exquisite backdrop for the historical buildings, museums and gardens of this 1,200-acre (486-ha) park. Start your visit from the main thoroughfare, El Prado (The Promenade). Here you'll find original exhibit halls from the 1915 Panama–California International Exposition, most notably the Casa del Prado. The Timken Museum of Art, a few blocks south, has interesting Russian icons among its exhibits.

At the park's center are several small museums: San Diego History Museum, Museum of Photographic Arts, Model Railroad Museum and Hall of Champions (sports). The nearby Reuben H. Fleet Space Theater and Science Center provides hands-on exhibits for youngsters. The Natural History Museum features exhibits of southwest desert and marine life, and at the end of the plaza are The Museum of Man (► 61) and the San Diego Museum of Art.

Visit any of the three stages of the Globe Theatre to see contemporary or Shakespearean plays, or enjoy a summer musical at The Starlight Bowl.

Simply stated, the **San Diego Zoo** (► 111 for practical information) is among the finest zoos in the world. The 100 acres (40ha) simulate the natural habitats of the 800 species living here, and allows expansive roaming of its 4,000 animals, which include the only pair of pandas in the US. The Children's Zoo offers close-up views. There are guided bus tours, as well as an aerial tramway that rises 170ft (52m) over the zoo's grottoes and mesas, providing a fine overview of the park.

59B2

1 mile (1.61km) north of downtown San Diego

619/239 0512

Daily 9–4.30 (4 in winter)

Restaurants, stands ($$)

7, 7A or 7B from downtown

Excellent

Moderate

Visitor Center sells multi-day passports to the park; free in-park tram

2
Catalina Island

Known as "The Island of Romance," Santa Catalina Island is a perfect blend of relaxed resort, pristine shoreline and untouched wilderness.

Discovered in 1542 by Juan Rodriguez Cabrillo, Santa Catalina (commonly called Catalina Island) is roughly 26 miles (42km) from the mainland. One of the eight California Channel Islands, it is 21 miles (34km) long and 8 miles (13km) wide. No cars are allowed on the island, so use the public transportation or rent the electric golf carts and bicycles available.

In 1811, the indigenous Gabrileño Indians were forced to resettle on the mainland, leaving the island that later became the private property of the Wrigley family, the chewing gum heirs. Today, 86 percent of the island is owned by the non-profit Santa Catalina Island Conservancy, established in 1972 to preserve the island's natural beauty. The island provides a welcome retreat from mainland crowds, with its silent beaches, water sports, picturesque pier and deep-sea fishing.

The 1929 Avalon Casino is the most famous building on the island, best known for its art deco ballroom, which in its heyday was host to many of the world's most famous orchestras and big bands. The Catalina Island Museum, on the first floor of the Casino, exhibits the island's history. The Wrigley Mansion, with its botanical gardens, and the Avalon Pier, in the middle of Avalon Bay, provide fine views of the interior hills and the breathtaking shoreline.

69D1

Visitors Center, Green Pier

310/510 1520

Daily 8–5

Restaurants ($$$)

Catalina Express 310/519 1212 or 800/618 5533; 1 hour each way; hourly from San Pedro or Long Beach.
Catalina Passenger Service 949/673 5245; 75 minutes each way; departs from Balboa Pavilion 9, returns 4.30

Helicopter Service from Island Express 800/228 2566; 15 minutes each way

Travel moderate; exhibits inexpensive

Cruise ship at Catalina Island

3
Disneyland Park

Disneyland sets the standard for theme parks. This "happiest place on earth" attracts 12 million visitors each year.

Children and adults alike are enchanted by the illusion and entertainment of "magic kingdom," opened in 1955. The 80-acre (32-ha) park is divided into eight sections, offering such diverse attractions as fantasy rides, musical performances, parades, restaurants and shops.

The turrets and spires of Sleeping Beauty Castle

© Disney Enterprises, Inc.

✝ 69D1

✉ 1313 Harbor Boulevard, Anaheim

☎ 714/781 4565

🕐 Summer Mon–Fri 9am–midnight (until 1am Sat); winter Mon–Fri 10–6 (until 9pm weekends, hols). Hours can vary, check first

♿ Very good; free strollers and wheelchairs

💲 Expensive

❓ Hours and prices subject to change; on busy days park at the Disneyland Hotel and ride the monorail to the park

A series of pastel-colored walkways lead from the central plaza at the end of Main Street, U.S.A. into the various themed areas, each with their own attractions. Mickey's Toontown brings out the kid in everyone; Adventureland offers a jungle boat ride and the charming "Tiki Room". New Orleans Square has a Mississippi steamwheeler, the "Pirates of the Caribbean" attraction and the "Haunted Mansion."

In Frontierland, you can career down Big Thunder Mountain Railroad on a runaway train or raft across to Tom Sawyer Island. Critter Country is the home of the "Splash Mountain" flume ride. Fantasyland begins when you cross the moat to Sleeping Beauty Castle, while Tomorrowland explores the future with attractions like "Space Mountain" and "Star Tours." For the courageous, the "Indiana Jones Adventure" takes you on a trek to the Temple of the Forbidden Eye. Disney characters roam the streets and pose for pictures. California Adventure Park, a celebration of the State's past and future, is next to Disneyland.

4
Golden Gate Bridge & National Recreation Area

The Golden Gate Bridge is quite easily the most beautiful and easily recognized bridge in the world.

The rust-colored symbol of the West Coast stands as a beacon at the entrance of San Francisco Bay. Built in 1937 it is beautiful and impressive from any angle. Often cloaked in fog, the bridge is extraordinarily graceful and delicate in design even though its overall length is 8,981ft (2,737m) and the stolid towers reach 746ft (227m) high. Connecting San Francisco to Marin County and northern California, the suspension bridge withstands winds of up to 100mph (161kph) and swings as much as 27ft (8m). Enjoy the drive over, or walk across for a truly spectacular perspective.

Golden Gate Park, the largest urban national park in the US, covers 74,000 acres (29,959ha) from San Mateo County to Tomales Bay. The giant recreation area offers many attractions, including Fort Mason on San Francisco's waterfront. A former military embarkation point for soldiers during World War II, today the fort is the site of museums, theaters, galleries, restaurants and the last unaltered, operational liberty ship, the SS *Jeremiah O'Brien*.

The Golden Gate Promenade is a scenic bayshore hike stretching 3.5 miles (5.5km) from Hyde Street Pier to Fort Point and beyond, across the Golden Gate Bridge. Among other sights in this impressive area are The Presidio, Baker Beach, Cliff House, Ocean Beach and Fort Funston, most of which are accessible by San Francisco's MUNI system.

✝ 28B5

Golden Gate Bridge

☎ MUNI 28; 415/554 6999 (hotline)

♿ Excellent

✋ Free northbound; southbound toll inexpensive

❓ Alcatraz tour info 415/705 5555

Recreation Area

✉ GGNRA, Building 201, Fort Mason, San Francisco, CA 94123

☎ 415/561 4700 (information line)

🕐 Mon–Fri 9.30–4.30

🍴 Cafés, stands ($)

♿ Excellent

✋ Moderate

Instantly recognizable— Golden Gate Bridge

5
Hearst Castle

68C2

750 Hearst Castle Road, San Simeon

805/927 2020 or 800/444 4445

Daily 8.20–3.20 (Dec start times may vary). Five different tours offered daily

Excellent

Moderate

214 miles (345km) southeast of San Francisco; 242 miles (390km) northwest of Los Angeles; parking just off Hwy 1 with shuttles buses to the castle. Four tours, priced separately. Tour 1 is recommended for first-time visitors. Reservations suggested

A rich man's castle—William Hearst's dream come true

William Randolph Hearst's tribute to excess and grandiosity crowns a hillside above the village of San Simeon.

The history of this fabulous castle dates back to 1865, when George Hearst purchased 40,000 acres (16,194ha) of Mexican land adjacent to San Simeon Bay. His son, newspaper magnate William Randolph, began the castle when he took possession of the land in 1919, which now numbers 250,000 acres (101,215ha). Using steamers and chain-driven trucks to transport materials to the remote spot, the palatial residence was not completed until 1947.

Casa Grande, as the mammoth mansion is called, boasts more than 100 rooms filled with priceless objects of art and antiques. It is one of seven estates owned by William Randolph, and was donated to the California Park Service in 1957.

Among the mansion's unique attributes are gothic fireplaces, Renaissance paintings (displayed in one of the 19 sitting rooms) and ceilings ranging in style from 16th-century Spanish to 18th-century Italian. In its prime, the doge's suite was reserved for the most important guests: presidents, visiting heads of state such as Winston Churchill and Hollywood luminaries. Marble colonnades and statuary flanking the indoor and outdoor pools replicate figures of antiquity.

There are also five greenhouses with over 700,000 annuals providing year-round color, tennis courts and a movie theater (in which Walt Disney hosted the first screening of *Snow White* in 1938). There are also two libraries, riding stables and the world's largest private zoo.

6
Hollywood

A one-time cow town, Hollywood is now the movie-making capital of the world and trend-setting center of glamour, glitter and excess.

The name that has drawn many a starry-eyed hopeful

Hollywood Boulevard is a relatively short street, but is one of the best known of all Los Angeles thoroughfares. Its wealth of art deco architecture has elevated it to the status of national historic district. From the 1920s to the 1950s, Hollywood boasted some of the country's largest movie palaces and exclusive department stores. As the movie industry expanded outward, Hollywood lost its luster, but the faded star is now staging a comeback.

The Hollywood Roosevelt Hotel (▶ 101), site of the first Academy Awards, has been renovated and displays historical film memorabilia throughout. An ambitious three-block redevelopment project around Sid Grauman's 1927 Chinese Theatre (now Mann's Chinese) offers shops, cinemas, restaurants and the Hollywood Studio Museum.

Hollywood abounds with guided bus tours of every sort. Walking tours of its bronze-starred Walk of Fame are extremely popular. Begun in 1960 with only eight stars, there are now close to 3,000 celebrity prints. The 1920s Hollywood sign can best be viewed by venturing up Beachwood Canyon on the eastern edge of Hollywood or from Griffith Observatory, high atop Mount Hollywood.

Paramount Studio provides a peek into the world of film-making. Free tickets to several popular TV shows are readily available outside Mann's Theatre or through the major network studios.

Hawkers along Sunset and Hollywood Boulevards offer surprisingly accurate maps to celebrity homes at a low price; you can drive yourself or take a bus tour.

 46B4

 Hollywood Visitors Bureau, 333 South Hope Street

Ⓒ 213/624 7300; 323/937 3661 (LA TOURS); 323/469 8311 (Hollywood Chamber of Commerce)

 Numerous restaurants, some open 24 hours ($–$$$)

7
Monterey Peninsula

✚ 68B3

✉ 122 miles (197km) southeast of San Francisco; 334 miles (539km) northwest of LA

☎ 831/649 1770 (Visitors Bureau); 831/649 7118 (State Historical Park); 831/624 2522 (Carmel Business Association); 831/659 0333 (Steinbeck Country Tours)

🍴 Various restaurants ($–$$$)

🚌 Monterey–Salinas Transit

✋ Inexpensive

Monterey Beach

"This is the California men dreamed of years ago. The face of the earth as the Creator intended it to look." Henry Miller

For more than 300 years the Monterey Peninsula has enchanted everyone who has seen it. Formed by the Monterey and Carmel bays, the peninsula juts into the Pacific Ocean 120 miles (194km) south of San Francisco. Pristine beaches, craggy rock formations and wind- and wave-warped cypresses make the area among the most popular scenic spots in the world.

Nowhere in California is the state's Latin heritage more prevalent than in Monterey, where its exquisitely restored adobe buildings give testimony to the Spanish and Mexican periods of California history.

From art galleries in Carmel (▶ 71) to the grand estates in the dense woods of the Del Monte Forest, the scenic 17-Mile Drive through the forest between Pacific Grove and Carmel is almost incomparable in beauty.

The legacy of famed California author John Steinbeck can be traced at The National Steinbeck Center in Salinas (open daily). You can also visit his preserved cottage in nearby Pacific Grove.

Carmel-by-the-Sea is an enchanting village. Much of its architecture is reminiscent of rural European and early California styles. Monterey's Fisherman's Wharf has a magnificent promenade of fish markets, shops and theaters. For a different perspective, a sail can be arranged aboard the restored tall ship *Californian*.

Established at the turn of the century by a group of writers and artists, Carmel was originally a planned resort. As its popularity soared, it took on the reputation of something completely different: an exclusive bohemian retreat. Resisting efforts for modernization, Carmel has preserved its idyllic setting. At Point Lobos State Reserve, 2 miles (3.5km) south of Carmel, harbor seals, gray whales and California sea lions frolic among a variety of sea birds and pelicans, a sight seen nowhere else in the world.

Sea lions are a familiar sight at Monterey

8
Napa Valley

Only 30 miles (48km) long and 3 miles (5km) across at its widest, this little valley boasts some 220 wineries.

Yountville, in the Napa Valley, is an important center of wine production

✝ 68B4

✉ Visitor Information Center, 1310 Napa Town Center, Napa, 94559

☎ 707/226 7459 (Visitor Information Center) 707/253 2111; 800/427 4124 (Napa Valley Wine Train)

🕐 Hours vary; some tours require reservations

🍴 Restaurants in the towns ($$–$$$)

✋ Free–inexpensive

Leader of the American wine industry, the Napa Valley boasts such well-known names as Robert Mondavi, Domaine Chandon, Beringer and Sterling. Although the greatest concentration of wineries is along State Route 29, north from Napa to Calistoga, knowledgeable travelers use the Silverado Trail, a scenic, vineyard-lined parallel road along the eastern edge of the valley.

The city of Napa is the largest, although each of the valley towns has its charms. In Calistoga there are spas and geysers, one of which shoots 60ft (18m) into the air every 40 minutes. St. Helena claims many of the region's best dining and lodging choices, as well as a wine library and the Silverado Museum. An ancient volcanic eruption from Washington's Mount St. Helens around 3 million years ago caused the giant redwoods of California to become instantly petrified. You'll find the Petrified Forest between Calistoga and Santa Rosa.

Outside of these towns lie more wineries, markets, inns, quiet picnic areas and historic parklands. Most visitors tour the vineyards, which offer a look at the wine-making process and feature wine-tastings, but there are also five different walking tours of the incredible architectural highlights of the valley (maps available at the information center). If possible, avoid the crowded summer weekends. Most vintners now charge a small fee for the tastings and a few require reservations.

9

Redwood National Park

*A vast forest of giant redwoods grows
naturally nowhere else in the country except in
this coastal region.*

Before California's famous gold rush, and the resulting
surge of new population, the world's tallest trees blanketed
an area 30 miles (48km) wide and 450 miles (726km) long.
The majority of today's redwood "stands" are along US
101, from Leggett north to Crescent City. It is about a five-
hour drive from San Francisco to the southern edge of the
Redwood Forest, via the scenic coastal highway.

A small segment of old growth redwoods and
outstanding coastal scenery have been protected in the
106,000-acre (42,915-ha) Redwood National Park. Eight
miles (13km) of shoreline roads and more than 150 miles
(242km) of trails afford close-up encounters with these
trees and the abundant plant and animal life they nurture.

The three main state
parks within the Park's
boundaries are Prairie
Creek, Del Norte Coast and
Jedediah Smith. Campers
favor Prairie Creek because
of its herds of native
Roosevelt elk and great
expansive beach (Gold
Bluffs Beach). Lady Bird
Johnson Cove is especially
beautiful. Don't miss the
Libby Tree, the tallest
known tree, which towers
to over 368ft (112m).

A drive through Del
Norte Coast park allows
you to enjoy spectacular
ocean views and the inland
forest simultaneously. The
giant redwoods grow
closest to the shoreline at
the Damnation Creek Trail.
In the spring, this area is
the best place to view the
abundant growth of rhodo-
dendrons and azaleas.

At the north end of the
park, the Jedediah Smith
terrain gives you an
elevated perspective.

☩ 68B6

✉ National Park
Headquarters, 1111
Second Street,
Crescent City, 95531

☎ 707/464 6101
(Redwood National Park
Information Center)

🍴 Restaurants ($); picnic
facilities

✋ Moderate

*Giant redwood—one of
the world's largest trees*

10
Yosemite National Park

✚ 69D4

✉ Yosemite Valley Visitors Center

☎ 209/372 0200

🕐 Apr–end May 9–6;
Jul–end Aug 8–8;
Sep–end Oct 8–6;
Nov–end Mar 9–5

🍴 Restaurants ($)

✋ Moderate

Winter lends its own special majesty to Yosemite National Park

By any standards, Yosemite is the most spectacular national park in the country. To call it awe-inspiring would be an understatement.

Nearly 70 percent of the annual visitors to Yosemite National Park arrive in the summer and stay within the compact but awesome Yosemite Valley. The main section of the park, just 7sq miles (18sq km) in area, boasts monumental granite walls and high-diving waterfalls, but there remains almost 1,200sq miles (3,076sq km) of splendor to explore. Beyond are such natural wonders as giant sequoias, alpine meadows, lakes and trout-filled streams, Glacier Point and majestic 13,000-ft (3,963-m) Sierra Nevada peaks. Giant sequoias are located in the Mariposa Grove, near the park's south entrance, about 30 miles (48km) from Yosemite Valley. In this great forest, over 200 trees measure more than 10ft (3m) in diameter.

Some of the park's finest scenery is in the wild back country along the Tioga Road. There are rustic lodges and campgrounds (permit camping). In the main valley, 3,500-ft (1,067-m) El Capitan attracts climbers from around the world.

Off-season visits are also spectacular. In fall, leaves turn from green to crimson and gold and nights are cool and pleasant. Spring offers magnificent waterfalls that create rainbows across the valley floor. For the ambitious, there's the 200-mile (322-km) John Muir Trail that follows the naturalist's path through the wilderness. For many, the winter provides solitude and restores the raw grandeur of the park. The ski season at Badger Pass lasts from the end of November until mid-April.

What
To See

Above: *Cable-car, San Francisco—
a fun way to travel around the city*

27

SAN FRANCISCO

0   1   2 km

- Bay Area Rapid Transit (BART) Stations
- 49 Mile Scenic Drive

GOLDEN GATE BRIDGE
Fort Point National Historic Site
Crissy Field
Golden Gate Promenade
MARINA BLVD
Palace of Fine Arts
PRESIDIO
Presidio Army Museum
Baker Beach
Golden Gate National Recreation Area
PRESIDIO HEIGHTS
San Francisco Fire Department Pioneer Memorial Museum

South Bay
Lands End
China Beach
Lincoln Park
Palace of the Legion of Honor
Holocaust Memorial
SEACLIFF
Point Lobos
Veterans Hospital
POINT LOBOS AVE
25TH AVENUE
CLEMENT STREET
GEARY BOULEVARD
ARGUELLO BLVD
PARK PRESIDIO BOULEVARD
TURK ST
MASONIC AVE
University of San Francisco
Seal Rocks
Cliff House
RICHMOND
FULTON STREET
de Young Museum
Ocean Beach
Golden Gate Park
Japanese Tea Garden
Stow Lake
Conservatory of Flowers
Panhandle
HAIGHT-ASHBURY
STANYAN STREET
Strybing Arboretum & Botanical Gardens
LINCOLN WAY
JUDAH STREET
PARNASSUS AVE
7TH AVENUE
BUENA VISTA
SUNSET
19TH AVENUE
ORTEGA STREET
Sunset Reservoir
FOREST HILL
Twin Peaks
GREAT HIGHWAY
SUNSET BOULEVARD
TARAVAL STREET
PARKSIDE
PORTOLA DRIVE
DIAMOND Gle
Mt Davidson 282m
Pine Lake Park
SLOAT
Sigmund Stern Grove
San Francisco Zoo
BOULEVARD
Stonestown Shopping Center
ST FRANCIS WOOD
GLEN PARK
OCEAN AVENUE
City College of San Francisco
SOUTHERN FREEWAY
Balboa Park
Harding Park
LAKE MERCED BLVD
San Francisco State University
INGLESIDE
Lake Merced
Golden Gate National Recreation Area
JOHN MUIR DRIVE
BROTHERHOOD WAY
OCEAN VIEW
SKYLINE BOULEVARD
San Francisco
DALY CITY
Daly City

A   B   C

Alcatraz Island

Hyde St
Pier
Fisherman's
Wharf
Pier 39

Yerba Buena
Island

Mexican Museum &
San Francisco Craft
& Folk Art Museum
arina
reen
Fort Mason
Maritime
Museum
The
Cannery
BAY ST
TELEGRAPH

MARINA
Ghirardelli
Square
SF Art
Institute
Coit Hill
Tower
NORTH
BEACH

RUSSIAN HILL
COLUMBUS AVE
THE EMBARCADERO
SAN FRANCISCO

OMBARD ST

Octagon
House
UNION ST
BROADWAY
Jackson
Square
Ferry Building

PACIFIC HEIGHTS
Haas-Lilienthal House
California
Historical Society
VAN NESS AVE
HYDE ST
Cable Car
Mus
NOB HILL
Grace
Cathedral
Transamerica Pyramid
Wells Fargo Museum
Chinatown
Embarcadero
OAKLAND BAY BRIDGE

CALIFORNIA STREET
POST ST
FINANCIAL
DI TRICT

Duquette
oundation of
avilion of
st Francis
Japantown
Union
Square
Powell
Montgomery Street
Museum of Modern Art

St Mary's
Cathedral
TENDERLOIN
Old US Mint
Moscone Center

WESTERN
ADDITION
Alamo
Square
Civic
Center
MARKET
HOWARD
SOUTH
OF
MARKET
California Academy
of Sciences

DIVISADERO
FELL ST
Civic
Center
4TH ST
SBC Park
(SF Giants)
China
Basin

STREET
LOWER
HAIGHT
US
Mint
19TH STREET
6TH ST
Hall of
Justice
San
Francisco
Bay

uena
ista
Park
14TH STREET
American
Indian Center
101
16TH STREET
280
Central
Basin

Mission
Dolores
CASTRO
16th Street
Mission
MISSION
POTRERO
HILL
3RD STREET
SOUTHERN EMBARCADERO FREEWAY

UREKA
VALLEY
CASTRO STREET
DOLORES STREET
GUERRERO STREET
MISSION STREET
San Francisco
General Hospital

CLIPPER STREET
24th Street Mission
ARMY STREET
JAMES LICK FREEWAY

NOE VALLEY
HEIGHTS
anyon
ark
101
BERNAL
HEIGHTS

SAN JOSE AVENUE
280
India
Basin

len Park
QUINT STREET
BAYSHORE
HUNTER'S
POINT

PORTOLA
3RD STREET
JAMES LICK FREEWAY
BAYVIEW

MISSION STREET
PERSIA AVENUE
EXCELSIOR
John
McLaren
Park
MANSELL STREET
San Francisco Bay
Naval Shipyard
South
Basin

GENEVA AVENUE
VISITACION
VALLEY
Bay View
Park
Monster Park
(49ers)
Candlestick
Park

ity Limit
Cow Palace
101
San Francisco
International Airport

D
E
F

San Francisco

Its location on one of the world's largest natural harbors, the San Francisco Bay, provides this city with some fabulous natural views to backdrop the prevalent Victorian architecture. From hippie-haven Haight-Ashbury to the touristy Fisherman's Wharf, San Francisco has retained its historical charm.

Ironically, the horrible earthquakes for which this city is infamously known have created its most unusual feature: the hilly, twisting streets. Lombard Street, in swank Russian Hill, is "the crookedest street in the world."

Cable-cars make city travel fun as well as practical, with three main lines: Powell and Market streets from downtown to Fisherman's Wharf, and along California Street from Embarcadero to Van Ness. Tickets may be purchased on board the cars.

> *"It is an odd thing, but anyone who disappears is said to be seen in San Francisco. "*
>
> **OSCAR WILDE**
> while giving a lecture to the
> Bohemian Club, San Francisco
> (December 1882)

San Francisco

The Gold Rush of the mid-19th century brought a diverse ethnicity to San Francisco. Areas like Chinatown and North Beach have preserved their different native cultures.

Out in the bay to the north is the infamous Alcatraz Island, the site of the notorious former prison. It is easily seen from Coit Tower, on top of Telegraph Hill. Russian Hill provides a panoramic look at the Golden Gate Bridge and the bay. To the north and east of the city lie the Napa Valley and Marin County, where wine-tasting is the hobby of choice.

Few places in the world can boast the sophistication of a major metropolitan area while also being offset by 42 hills and, and at the same time, surrounded by the serenity of lush vineyards as does San Francisco.

Famously crooked Lombard Street

31

What to See in San Francisco

ALCATRAZ ✪✪✪

Of the 14 islands punctuating the massive San Francisco Bay, 12-acre (5-ha) Alcatraz is the most famous. Rising 135ft (41m) out of the bay, it is easy to see why it is nicknamed "The Rock." Although wild flowers are abundant on the island and the views of the bay and the Golden Gate bridge are breathtaking, most visitors visit the

Alcatraz can be reached by a short ferry crossing from Fisherman's Wharf

➕ 29D6
☎ 415/705 5555
⏱ Hours vary, advance reservations recommended
🚢 Ferry from Pier 41, Fisherman's Wharf
🏷 Moderate

island to tour the massive fortress that covers most of the grounds. Built in 1858 as a military post, it soon became a military prison and finally a federal penitentiary.

Because of the severe tides and undertow of the surrounding chilly waters, escape from the prison was reputed to be impossible. Three inmates dug their way out of their prison cells and disappeared in 1962. No one knows if they made it to the mainland, but their bodies were never found. The prison closed soon after the attempt, and a group of Native Americans claimed the island as their birthright. Some of the buildings were burned before the National Park Service took control and reopened Alcatraz as a tourist attraction in 1973.

Three prominent movies have been filmed on the island: *Escape from Alcatraz*, *The Birdman of Alcatraz* and *The Rock*. Tours include a close-up look at the cells with audio-cassette narration by former prisoners and guards and exterior trail walks led by park rangers. Dress warmly and wear comfortable shoes.

Stone exhibit in the Asian Art Museum

ASIAN ART MUSEUM ✪✪

More than 40 Asian countries are represented in this museum, the largest of its kind outside the Asian continent. Exclusive to this museum are works of Asian art spanning 4,000 years of Chinese history. It also houses outstanding exhibits from India, Japan and Korea and more than 300 works from the estates of Chinese emperors. The msueum moved from its Golden Gate Park location to a grand, renovated space in the Civic Center in 2003.

www.asianart.org
✚ 29D4
✉ 200 Larkin Street, Civic Center
☎ 415/581 3500
🕐 Tue–Sun 10–5, Thu 10–9
💵 Moderate, free 1st Tue of month

CABLE CAR MUSEUM AND POWERHOUSE VIEWING GALLERY ✪✪

If you're fascinated by San Francisco's cable-cars, visit this working nerve center and museum. On exhibit are the first cable-cars, which went unchanged for almost 100 years. Their design was modernized in 1982. Also housed in the three-level, red-brick 1907 barn are photographs, artifacts and a model collection. From the viewing gallery you can watch craftsmen working on the cars.

✚ 29E5
✉ 1201 Mason Street
☎ 415/474 1887
🕐 Daily 10–5 (extended hours in spring and summer)
💵 Free

CALIFORNIA ACADEMY OF SCIENCES ✪✪✪

Dating back to the mid-19th century, this is considered one of the finest natural history museums in the world. It houses several galleries, an exhibit that allows visitors to "experience" an earthquake, and a hands-on Discovery Room for children. The Steinhart Aquarium has almost 14,000 salt-water species which include octopuses, sea-horses, dolphins and sharks. The ANTS exhibit showcases the nest building and food collecting behavior of six live ant colonies. The Howard Street location also has a nurturing place called the Nature Nest for young visitors. Note: The Academy has moved to temporary premises in Howard Street and is expected to return to Golden Gate Park in 2008.

✚ 29E4
✉ 875 Howard Street, between 4th and 5th streets
☎ 415/750 7145
🕐 Daily 10–5 (extended hours in summer)
💵 Moderate; senior/children rates. Free 1st Wed of month

✛ 28A5
✉ 34th Avenue and Clement Street, Lincoln Park
☎ 415/750 3600
🕐 Tue–Sun 9.30–5
💵 Moderate; senior/children rates; free every Tue

---

www.cartoonart.org
✛ 29D3
✉ 655 Mission Street
☎ 415/227 8666
🕐 Tue–Sun 11–5. Closed holidays
💵 Moderate; senior/children rates

✛ 29D5
✉ 965 Clay Street
☎ 415/391 1188
🕐 Tue–Fri noon–5, Sat–Sun noon–4
💵 Inexpensive

✛ 29D4
✉ Van Ness Avenue/Polk Street at Grove and McAllister streets
☎ 415/554 4858 (information); 415/554 4933 (tour manager)
💵 Free

City Hall epitomizes the Beaux-Arts style

CALIFORNIA PALACE OF THE LEGION OF HONOR

Refurbished in 1995, this classical palace was inspired by the Hotel de Salm in Paris, the site where Napoleon established the Legion D'Honneur. The Palace houses an extraordinary collection of 75,000 prints and drawings from the Achenbach Foundation, and expansive European art dating from 2500BC through to the 20th century. Rodin's *The Thinker* is on display in the courtyard.

CARTOON ART MUSEUM

This museum houses permanent and rotating exhibits of original two- and three-dimensional art and cartoon objects. You can see the original artwork and drawings used in the production of cartoons. Some exhibits go back to the 18th century. Video presentations are also part of the program.

CHINESE HISTORICAL SOCIETY OF AMERICA

The largest collection of Chinese-American objects in the US is housed here, including Chinese dragon heads, an 1880 Buddhist altar and a concise history of the Chinese experience in America, from 1840 to the present day.

CIVIC CENTER PLAZA

Dominated by the French Renaissance-inspired City Hall, the complex dates back to the 1906 earthquake. On the west end is the War Memorial and Performing Arts Center. The Center is home to the Louise M. Davies Symphony Hall, the War Memorial Opera House and the War Memorial Veterans Building. The latter contains the San Francisco Museum of Modern Art and the Herbst Theatre, where the United Nations charter was signed in 1945. Other classically styled buildings in the plaza complex are the Civic Auditorium, the San Francisco Public Library and the State Building.

A Walk Around Chinatown

This walk takes you through the largest Chinese community outside Asia.

Enter through the Chinatown Gate, at Bush Street and Grant Avenue.

Note the dragon-entwined lampposts and pagoda roofs as you are greeted by a cacophony of Chinese street merchants and the aromas of simmering noodles.

Walk north on Grant to the Dragon House Antiques (No. 455).

Continue up Grant to St. Mary's Park where there's a 12-ft (3.5-m) sculpture of Sun Yat-sen.

Continue north to Clay, turn right to Kearny, then left to Portsmouth Square. Across Kearny is the Holiday Inn.

Pop inside to the Chinese Cultural Center.

Go north on Kearny, to Pacific, then left to the New Asia restaurant (No. 772).

This is a good choice for lunch.

Continue east on Pacific to Grant, then go left two blocks to Washington. Turn right.

Admire the three-tiered pagoda-style Bank of Canton, then continue west to the Tien Hou Temple (in Waverly Place on Washington). Around the corner is The Great China Herb Co. (No. 857), for herbal prescriptions.

Continue west on Washington to Stockton, then turn left.

The Chinese Six Companies building (No. 843) is an architectural wonder, with its curved roof tiles and elaborate cornices.

Walk south on Stockton to the Stockton Street Tunnel. A 15-minute walk through the tunnel brings you to downtown Union Square.

Distance
5 miles (8km)

Time
2–4 hours

Start point
Chinatown Gate
✚ 29E5

End point
Union Square
✚ 29E5

Lunch
New Asia ($$)
✉ 772 Pacific Avenue
☎ 415/391 6666

Chinatown lion

29D6
North of North Beach
Cafés, stands ($)
Excellent

28B5
GGNRA, Building 201, Fort Mason, San Francisco, CA 94123
415/561 4700; 415/752 4227 (Japanese Tea Garden)
Cafés, stands ($)
Excellent
Moderate

FISHERMAN'S WHARF

Bustling Fisherman's Wharf is the center of San Francisco's thriving tourist trade. It has many shops, street stands, food emporia and the like. Originally, it was an active base for San Francisco Bay's once busy fishing industry, until the late 1940s. A small fleet still operates.

GOLDEN GATE NATIONAL RECREATION AREA

This huge area takes in Golden Gate Park with its museums, open-air performances and sporting events (► 19). Once an expanse of sand dunes, the area has been transformed into a botanical masterpiece. The Strybing Arboretum and Botanical Gardens near the museum complex encompass 70 acres (28ha) of plant life. The Japanese Tea Garden, with koi ponds and an 18th-century Buddha, is one of the most interesting spots in all San Francisco. The children's playground has a working carousel, and the park is host to dozens of cultural fairs and exhibits, and also food- and wine-tastings. In summer, there are operas and a popular Shakespearean festival.

Near the Golden Gate Bridge, the historical Fort Mason Center, once an embarkation point for American soldiers, houses a youth hostel, several theaters, the African-American Historical and Cultural Society, the Museo Italo-Americano, the Mexican Museum (due to move location) and the SS *Jeremiah O'Brien*. A Golden Gate Explorer Pass provides unlimited admission to all museums and gardens for six months.

The Japanese Tea Garden at Golden Gate Park

Did you know ?

For thousands of years, the only inhabitants near the current Golden Gate region were the Native American Ohlones, a sub-tribe of the Coast Miwok. Feasting mainly on oysters, they left huge piles of the shells which can still be seen. The largest pile is located at Coyote Hills, in southern Alameda County.

GRACE CATHEDRAL 😊😊

Taking over a half-century to build, this marvellous structure is a near-perfect replica of a Florentine cathedral. The singing of the Vespers each Thursday at 5.15pm is a truly spiritual experience.

🚩 29E5
✉ 1100 California Street
☎ 415/749 6300
💵 Free, but donations accepted

HYDE STREET PIER AND HISTORICAL SHIPS 😊

In the Fisherman's Wharf area, this pier is the permanent home of several historical ships. Here you will find the ferry boat *Eureka* (1890), once the world's largest ferry boat, and the *Balclutha*, a square-rigged sailing ship from Scotland (1886), famed for rounding Cape Horn several times. Before leaving the area, drop into the National Maritime Museum at nearby Aquatic Park.

🚩 29D6
☎ 415/561 7100
🕐 Daily 10–5
💵 Inexpensive. National Park Golden Eagle Pass free

LOMBARD STREET 😊😊😊

Located in the Russian Hill district, this is San Francisco's famous "crookedest" street. Traffic zigzags down it at 5mph (8kph), moving around colorful gardens which were established in the 1920s.

🚩 29D5
✉ Between Hyde and Leavenworth streets

MISSION SAN FRANCISCO DE ASIS (MISSION DOLORES) 😊😊😊

Founded in 1776 and moved to its present site in 1782, the mission is thought to be the oldest standing structure in the city. Adjoining is the Mission Dolores Basilica, the least changed of all California's existing missions. The architecture of Mission Dolores is a combination of Moorish, Mission and Corinthian styles, and the garden cemetery is filled with the burial sites of San Francisco pioneers.

🚩 29D4
✉ 16th and Dolores streets
☎ 415/621 8203
🕐 Daily 9–4.30 (until 4 in fall and winter)
💵 Inexpensive

Stained glass at Mission Dolores, the sixth of 21 Missions founded by the Spanish in California

⊕ 28C4
✉ 2501 Irving Street (at 26th Avenue)
☎ 415/750 3600
🕐 Tue–Sat 10–4.45
✋ Free

⊕ 68B3
✉ West Cliff Drive
☎ 831/423 4609
🕐 Beach daily 8–dusk; visitor center 10–4
✋ Inexpensive

⊕ 29E5

Coit Tower
☎ 415/362 0808
🕐 Daily 10–6.30
🕐 Inexpensive (to go to top of tower)

DE YOUNG MUSEUM   ✪✪✪
Reopened in 2005 as the de Young Museum, the museum contains a collection of American artwork in a 22-gallery complex set in Golden Gate Park. The museum's exhibits include paintings, sculpture, decorative arts, textiles and furniture. Some of the artwork dates to the mid-17th century. Also on display are classical and tribal works.

NATURAL BRIDGES STATE BEACH   ✪
Set in 65 acres (26ha), this beach, just before Santa Cruz, is a wonderful place to observe the migration of the colorful Monarch butterfly between mid-October and February. There are also tide pools to explore, as well as ecological and wildlife exhibits in the visitor center.

NORTH BEACH   ✪✪✪
This thriving, trendy neighborhood, on the northeastern tip of San Francisco, is bound by Chinatown, the Financial District and Russian Hill. North Beach has a distinctly Italian atmosphere, and is central to most attractions, shops and restaurants in the area. Its heyday in the 1950s saw Jack Kerouac and other Beat Generation poets frequenting the cafés and bookstores, which remain important cultural meeting places. At the center of the neighborhood is **Coit Tower**, an impressive 210-ft (64-m) landmark, built in 1934, reached on foot via the Filbert Steps by Darnell Place.

The Palace of Fine Arts, designed as a Roman ruin, incorporates a classical domed rotunda as its centerpiece

⊕ 28C5
✉ 3601 Lyon Street
☎ 415/561 0360
🕐 Tue–Sun 10–5; open on Mon hols
✋ Moderate, free 1st Wed of month

PALACE OF FINE ARTS   ✪✪
This Bernard Maybeck Greco-Romanesque rotunda is one of the most photographed buildings in San Francisco. Levelled by the great earthquake of 1906, it was completely rebuilt in 1915 and today presents continuing cultural events. Inside the complex is the Exploratorium, a wonderful hands-on science museum, ideal for families, with toys disguised as science education.

ST. MARY'S CATHEDRAL OF THE ASSUMPTION ✪✪✪

The radical architecture by Pietro Belluschi and Pier Luigi Nervi caused great debate during construction. Rising on concrete pylons to a height of 190ft (58m), the exterior resembles a washing machine agitator. Inside, however, the soaring cruciform is nothing short of breathtaking. The majestic pipe organ, itself, is worth seeing.

✛ 29D4
⊠ 1111 Gough Street
☎ 415/567 2020
⏲ Mon–Fri 7–5, Sun 7–6.30
✋ Free, but donations accepted

SFMOMA: One of the finest museums of modern art in the country

SAN FRANCISCO MUSEUM OF MODERN ART ✪✪✪

Devoted solely to modern art and occupying a quarter-million sq ft, this is the main structure in the Yerba Buena Arts Center (SoMo district). Exhibits include a world-renowned collection of photography, and 20th-century works from such artists as Dali, O'Keefe and Jasper Johns. A current feature exhibit is "From Matisse to Diebenkorn: Works from the Permanent Collection."

✛ 29E5
⊠ 151 Third Street
☎ 415/357 4000
⏲ Mon, Tue, Fri–Sun 11–5.45; Thu 11–8.45
✋ Moderate, senior/student rates, free 1st Tue of month

SAUSALITO ✪

This is the first small town in Marin County after crossing the Golden Gate Bridge. Once a fishing town, it has unfortunately been overrun with tacky tourist shops and no longer has the great charm of years past.

✛ 68B4
⊠ 5 miles (8km) north of San Francisco
🚢 Ferry from Ferry Building or Fisherman's Wharf

TRANSAMERICA PYRAMID ✪✪

Depending on who you ask, this structure is either a landmark or an eyesore. Completed in 1972, the pyramid skyscraper juts 853ft (260m) skyward, making it the tallest building in San Francisco.

✛ 29E5
⊠ 600 Montgomery Street
⏲ Mon–Fri 8–4

Food & Drink

Because of its immensely diverse cultural make-up, California is a food lover's paradise. The major cities have authentic cuisine from almost every nation in the world.

Cuisine

Nearby Mexico exerts a strong influence, especially encouraging the generous use of avocados and salsa. There are tacquerias everywhere. Cilantro is the spice of choice.

Sushi is fresh and popular. Chinese food, especially in San Francisco's Chinatown, is excellent. Fine dining establishments in the major cities feature delicious French cuisine.

All along the Coast are seafood houses to fit every budget. Fresh tuna and black cod are popular, while crab, oysters and jumbo shrimp cocktails satisfy lighter appetites.

North Beach in San Francisco has the best

Below: *Crab vendor on Fisherman's Wharf*
Right: *Delicious seafood dishes are on offer all along the coast*

authentic Italian food, pasta can be found everywhere, Beverly Hills has great Jewish delis and Solvang (Central Coast) features fine Scandinavian food.

Most visitors to the area, however, look forward to sampling genuine California cuisine. Menus are renowned for catering to swimsuit figures by being light, healthy and diet-friendly. For vegetarians, there is a huge year-round variety of locally grown vegetables (steamed), fresh salads with gourmet greens, and fresh fruits. Non-meat burgers and chicken are popular. The finest steaks can also be found, especially around the northern farming areas.

For a busy day of sightseeing, there are literally thousands of fast-food establishments. Even most of the small, inland towns have the major chains. In-N-Out Burger is a good choice for those on the run.

Lori's Diner—a popular venue

Beverages

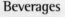

Health-conscious Californians consume more bottled water per capita than any other state in the US. This may be due to the fact that a large part of the state has a desert-like climate and bottled water is easy to carry. Restaurants and markets offer a wide selection of both carbonated and uncarbonated types. Especially in the Palm Springs area, there are many roadside stands offering tasty "date shakes."

Although there are a few local breweries, imported beers seem to be favored by the locals, so you can find almost any of the popular brands. Mexico's Corona is a top choice. Micro-breweries are also popular, so check out some of the local beer-bistros for thirst-quenching treats.

The Mexican margarita is a time-tested standard. The martini is said to have originated in San Francisco and the Mai Tai cocktail was invented at Trader Vic's, at the original location in Oarkland.

Wine is said to appease and to have dietary and health considerations. Because so much excellent wine is produced in the state, the selection is overwhelming and costs are relatively affordable. Wineries of great renown include Mondavi, Beringer, Domaine Chandon, Louis M. Martini, Buena Vista, Sebastiani and Korbel Champagne. A favorite is Mondavi's unfiltered Cabernet Sauvigon, while Pinot Noirs and Syrahs are also becoming increasingly popular. Along with the world-famous Napa Valley and Sonoma wines, the wineries of the central coastal area are gaining in prominence.

Star Gazing
When dining and drinking in LA, remember that "star-gazing" may not necessarily be an exercise in astronomy. You could find yourself rubbing elbows with a celebrity straight off the screen as you satisfy your appetite. There is year-round patio dining, and casual attire is the norm. Most establishments accept all major credit cards.

Californian wines are in a class of their own

29D5

Octagon House
- ✉ 2645 Gough Street
- ☎ 415/441 7512
- ⏰ 2nd and 4th Thu and 2nd Sun of each month (except Jan), noon–3. Closed holidays
- 💰 Contributions

68B3
- ✉ Bay and High Street
- ☎ 831/459 4008
- ⏰ Student-led tours Mon–Fri 10.30, 1.30
- 💰 Free, parking inexpensive

29E5
- ✉ 420 Montgomery Street
- ☎ 415/396 2619
- ⏰ Mon–Fri 9–5. Closed bank holidays
- 💰 Free

UNION STREET ✪✪✪

Union Street runs east–west from Montgomery Street in North Beach to the Presidio. It is one of the city's most fashionable areas in which to live and shop, and with its many beautifully restored Victorian mansions that have been converted into boutiques, art galleries and cafés, it is a must-see. Scattered among the bustling retail spots are several landmarks that should not be missed. The **Octagon House** (just off Union Street) is a pale-blue, eight-sided structure that features antique furniture from the 18th and 19th centuries. Also of interest is an exhibit containing the signatures of 54 of the 56 original signatories of the Declaration of Independence.

UNIVERSITY OF CALIFORNIA AT SANTA CRUZ ✪

On the campus are the remains of several buildings from the Cowell Ranch, dating back to the mid-19th century. Other outstanding buildings include two art galleries and the Long Marine Aquarium. The most popular exhibit in the aquarium is a virtually flawless skeleton of a blue whale. Eight colleges make up this 2,000-acre (810-ha) site, overlooking Monterey Bay and Santa Cruz.

WELLS FARGO HISTORY MUSEUM ✪✪

Located in the Wells Fargo Bank Building, the museum contains artifacts from the Old West and the California Gold Rush, and records the rise and fall of the company. There is a superbly preserved stagecoach and other interesting pieces from early years to the present.

A Drive Through Marin County

This drive takes you through scenic Marin County.

Begin at the Presidio in north San Francisco. Cross the Golden Gate Bridge and continue north on Highway 101.

Sausalito (➤ 39) is to your left.

Proceed north to the Tamalpais Valley exit and follow the signs to Muir Woods National Monument.

Here you can enjoy the beauty of the redwoods.

A dramatic panorama unfolds from the summit of Mount Tamalpais

Return to the 101 and continue northward.

Stop at the Marin County Civic Center, an architectural masterpiece designed by Frank Lloyd Wright in 1957.

Backtrack along the 101, through San Rafael, to Highway 580. Follow it across the Richmond–San Rafael Bridge.

Right before the bridge is San Quentin Prison. As you cross the bridge, San Francisco Bay is on your right and San Pablo Bay on your left.

A short distance past the bridge, take the 80 Freeway south to Berkeley.

Sites to see on the University of Berkeley campus include the Botanical Garden, Lawrence Hall of Science and the Phoebe Apperson Hearst Museum of Anthropology.

Continuing back on the 80 southbound, follow the highway past Emeryville and across the San Francisco–Oakland Bay Bridge.

Look right to see Treasure Island Naval Station and Alcatraz (➤ 32).

Take the first exit off the bridge to Fisherman's Wharf.

Distance
120 miles (194km)

Time
6–8 hours, depending on time spent at attractions

Start point
The Presidio
✚ 28C5

End point
Fisherman's Wharf
✚ 29D6

Lunch
Dipsea Cafe ($$)
✉ 200 Shoreline Highway/Highway 1, Mill Valley
☎ 415/381 0298
🕐 Daily 7am–3pm
also at
✉ 2200 Fourth Street, San Rafael
☎ 415/459 0700
🕐 Daily 7am–3pm

43

Los Angeles

Whether you come for the beaches, mountains, museums or movie stars, Los Angeles teems with activity. Bring your sunglasses and your tanning lotion because here in California there is plenty of sunshine. For dedicated sun-seekers, beautiful beaches stretch along the western edge of this seemingly endless metropolis. Zuma Beach is one of the best for enjoying the pastime made famous by the music of The Beach Boys—surfing.

At Venice Beach you can either stroll barefoot along the beach or join the hustle along the Boardwalk, where vendors hawk their souvenirs. This is home to some of the nation's most colorful characters: musicians, magicians and mime artists, as well as Muscle Beach body builders.

"Call Los Angeles any dirty name you like—Six Suburbs in Search of a City, Paradise with a Lobotomy, anything—but the fact remains that you are already living in it before you get there."

AUSTRALIAN CRITIC
CLIVE JAMES,
London Observer (1979)

———————— ● ————————

A distinctive LA landmark, the folk art extravaganza of Watts Towers

Mission San Fernando Rey de Espana

Six Flags Magic Mountain & William S Hart Park

Verdugo Mountains

VAN NUYS

NORTH HOLLYWOOD

BURBANK

Descanso Gardens

GOLDEN STATE FREEWAY

San Fernando Valley

VENTURA FREEWAY

NBC Studios

SHERMAN OAKS

Forest Lawn Memorial Park

Universal Studios Hollywood

Gene Autry Western Heritage Musem

GLENDALE

Norton Simon Museum of Art

Griffith Park

LA Zoo

Hollywood Griffith Park Planetarium

Southwest Museum

Heritage Square

SANTA MONICA MOUNTAIN

WEST HOLLYWOOD

BEVERLY HILLS

Mann's Chinese Theatre

Hollywood Wax Museum

Hollywood Bowl

Hollywood Studio Museum

Hollywood Memorial Park

Dodger Stadium

SAN DIEGO FREEWAY

Museum of Television & Film

Paramount Studios

Farmers Market

UCLA

LA County Museum of Art

La Brea Tar Pits & George C Page Museum

HOLLYWOOD FREEWAY

Chinatown

Music Center

El Pueblo de Los Angeles State Historical Park

Little Tokyo

Will Rogers State Historic Park

SANTA MONICA

Getty Center

Century City

SANTA MONICA FREEWAY

LOS ANGELES

City Hall

Museum of Contemporary Art

Malibu

Petersen Automotive Museum

CULVER CITY

Wells Fargo History Museum

Exposition Park (California Museum of Science & Industry, Los Angeles County Natural History Museum)

Memorial Coliseum & Sports Arena

MAYWOOD

HUNTINGTON PARK

Venice Beach

VENICE

Marina del Rey

PLAYA DEL REY

INGLEWOOD

HARBOR FREEWAY

Los Angeles International Airport

Watts Towers

SOUTH GATE

Los Angeles River

Santa Monica Bay

WESTMONT

LYNWOOD

HAWTHORNE

WILLOWBROOK

GARDENA

COMPTON

LONG BEACH FREEWAY

MANHATTAN BEACH

HERMOSA BEACH

REDONDO BEACH

SAN DIEGO FREEWAY

CARSON

TORRANCE

South Coast Botanic Garden

Palos Verdes Peninsula

Wayfarers' Chapel

WILMINGTON

LONG BEACH

RANCHO PALOS VERDES

Marineland

SAN PEDRO

San Pedro Bay

LOS ANGELES

0   5   10 km

A   B   C

San Gabriel Mountains

Angeles National Forest

San Gabriel
Reservoir

ALTADENA

MONROVIA

Morris
Reservoir

PASADENA

COLORADO FREEWAY

Tournament House
& Wrigley Gardens

Los Angeles State
& County Arboretum

GLENDORA

AZUSA

210

Huntington
Library &
Art Gallery/
Botanical
Gardens

SAN
GABRIEL

ARCADIA

Mission San
Gabriel Archangel

TEMPLE
CITY

BALDWIN
PARK

COVINA

605

ALHAMBRA

EL MONTE

SAN BERNARDINO FREEWAY

210

10

ROSEMEAD

WEST COVINA

MONTEREY
PARK

60

San Jose Hills

San Gabriel River

EAST LOS
ANGELES

RIVER FREEWAY

LA PUENTE

WALNUT

DIAMOND
BAR

POMONA

MONTEBELLO

60 FREEWAY

Hills

5

PICO
RIVERA

HACIENDA
HEIGHTS

ROWLAND
HEIGHTS

57

SAN GABRIEL

BELL
GARDENS

WHITTIER

Puente

DOWNEY

SOUTH
WHITTIER

LA HABRA

BREA

FREEWAY

PARAMOUNT

LA MIRADA

NORWALK

SANTA ANA

ORANGE

BELLFLOWER

YORBA
LINDA

CERRITOS

FULLERTON

PLACIENTA

Movieland Wax Museum

LAKEWOOD

91

605

Coyote Creek

BUENA PARK

ANAHEIM

Knott's
Berry Farm

CYPRESS

STANTON

Disneyland

5

Anaheim
Stadium

ORANGE

GARDEN
GROVE

55

Santa Ana River

WESTMINSTER

Bowers
Museum

SAN DIEGO

605

SANTA ANA

HUNTINGTON
BEACH

FOUNTAIN
VALLEY

Movieland
of the Air

Laguna Beach &
Art Museum,
& Newport Beach

FREEWAY

D

E

F

Los Angeles

Probably best known as the home of Hollywood, LA is a haven for the famous and those who never quite made it. Buy a map and take a self-guided driving tour past the homes of some of Hollywood's most famous residents.

One of Hollywood's landmark hotels

 46A4

✉ Visitors Bureau, 239 S Beverly Drive, Beverly Hills 90212

☎ 310/248 1015

What to See in Los Angeles

BEVERLY HILLS ✪✪✪

The City of Stars is the place where shopping and the entertainment industry each vie for their place as the number one attraction (➤ 49). Here you will find some of the most expensive real estate in the country. The city's most recognizable zip code (90210) receives more than 14 million visitors a year, making it the most popular destination in Los Angeles.

Beverly Hills has several main thoroughfares, all running east to west: Sunset Boulevard, at the north end, roughly splits the commercial and residential areas. Wilshire Boulevard is the main thoroughfare to the business and commercial centers. At the south end, Pico Boulevard marks the Beverly Hills border. This incorporated city has its own police and fire departments and its own library, complete with gold-colored library cards.

✚ 46C4

✉ 900 block of Broadway

CHINATOWN ✪✪

The cultural center of this unique community is home to about 5 percent of LA's 200,000 Chinese residents. Chinatown encompasses 16 square blocks, and its downtown area is filled with Asian architecture, good restaurants and import shops. The Kong Chow Temple is exquisite.

✚ 46C4

✉ 200 N Spring Street

☎ 213/978 0721

🕐 Mon–Fri 9–4

 Free

CITY HALL ✪

This building was the first skyscraper to be built in Los Angeles and served as The Daily Planet Building in the *Superman* television series of the 1950s. Guided tours are free—weekdays from 10am–1pm—and last 45 minutes. There is an observation deck on the 27th floor.

A Walk Around Beverly Hills

This walk begins on one of the most expensive shopping streets in the world.

Walk north from Wilshire on Rodeo Drive.

Do a spot of window-shopping in Tiffany's, Saks and other high end boutiques (➤ 107).

Proceed north several blocks to Little Santa Monica, then go east (right) a couple of blocks to Crescent.

On the corner of Crescent you'll see the historic former Beverly Hills Post Office and the magnificent Beverly Hills Municipal Building. The latter houses City Hall and the Beverly Hills library and police station.

Take a left on Crescent and proceed north across Santa Monica Boulevard and through the Beverly Hills "flatlands."

The homes along here are absolutely gorgeous.

At Sunset Boulevard, walk across to the newly restored Beverly Hills Hotel (➤ 101).

Take a few minutes to stroll through the splendid lobby.

Proceed east on Sunset to the West Hollywood business district.

Here you will pass the famous Roxy theater, Spago restaurant and The Whiskey A Go-Go.

Continue east, stopping for lunch at the chic Sunset Plaza, then on to Sunset. Turn right on Crescent Heights Road and go south to Melrose Avenue. Turn left on to Melrose and walk several blocks to Fairfax Avenue.

At this corner is the sprawling CBS Television City. Tours are available, as well as free tickets to live tapings of television shows.

South of CBS is the Farmers' Market and the Grove, where your tour ends.

Distance
4 miles (6.5km)

Time
3–4 hours, depending on time spent at attractions

Start point
Beverly Hills, corner of Wilshire and Rodeo
✚ 46A4

End point
Farmers' Market and the Grove complex of shops, restaurants and movie theaters
✚ 46A4

Lunch
Chin Chin ($)
✉ 8618 Sunset Boulevard
☎ 310/652 1818

Farmers' Market is a mix of fruit and vegetable stalls, souvenir shops and food stands

49

A street market in El Pueblo State Historic Park

🗺 46C5
✉ 1418 Descanso Drive, La Cañada Flintridge
☎ 818/949 4200
🕐 Daily 9–4.30. Closed Christmas Day
🎫 Moderate, special discounts

🗺 46C4
✉ Betweeen Alameda, Arcadia, Spring and Macy streets
☎ 213/628 1274
🕐 Hours vary call for information
🎫 Free

🗺 46B4

California Museum of Science and Industry
✉ Exposition Boulevard at Figueroa
☎ 213/744 7400
🕐 Daily 10–5
🎫 Free, charge for IMAX

California Afro-American Museum
☎ 213/744 7432
🕐 Wed–Sat 10–4
🎫 Free ($6 parking fee)

LA County Museum of Natural History
☎ 213/763 3466
🕐 Mon–Fri 9.30–5, Sat, Sun 10–5
🎫 Moderate, free first Tue of month

DESCANSO GARDENS ✪✪
These glorious gardens cover 65 acres (26ha), including a 30-acre (12-ha) California live oak forest. Over 100,000 camellias collected from around the world florish here, as do many roses, lilacs and other blossoms. The Japanese Garden has a serene teahouse. It is worth the short drive north of the city.

EL PUEBLO DE LOS ANGELES STATE ✪✪
HISTORICAL PARK
Here, on 44 acres (18ha) near downtown, you can visit the Avila Adobe (the oldest adobe house), Masonic Hall, Old Plaza Church and Sepulveda House. Founded in 1781, the main attraction for most visitors is Olvera Street, an open-air Mexican-style market place lined with specialty shops, vendors, cafés and restaurants.

EXPOSITION PARK ✪✪✪
The Los Angeles Memorial Coliseum was host to the Olympics in 1932 and 1984. Several museums are contained within, including the **California Museum of Science and Industry**, with interactive exhibits, Aerospace Complex and the surround-vision IMAX theater, featuring a five-story-high screen. Other museums include the **California Afro-American** and the **Los Angeles County Museum of Natural History,** with three floors of dinosaur, fossil and cultural exhibits.

> ### Did you know ?
>
> *Comedian Robin Williams said of Hollywood, "Living in Hollywood is like being in high school—only with money."*

FOREST LAWN MEMORIAL PARK ✪✪

A cemetery may seem like an unusual attraction, but there are 300 lush acres (121ha) of grounds here, with reproductions of such works as da Vinci's *Last Supper*, and the world's largest religious painting on canvas, Jan Styke's *The Crucifixion*. Also not to be missed are the ornate tombstones of celebrities and the beautiful gardens. Forest Lawn cemetery is the final resting place of such Hollywood film legends as Humphrey Bogart, Errol Flynn, Spencer Tracy, Stan Laurel, Carole Lombard, W. C. Fields, Jean Harlow and Cary Grant.

✚ 46B5
✉ 1712 South Glendale Avenue, Glendale
☎ 818/241 4151
🕐 Daily 8–5
✋ Free

Statue in Forest Lawn Memorial Park

THE GETTY CENTER ✪✪✪

Opened in December 1997, this billion-dollar arts complex sits high on a hill off the 405 San Diego freeway to the north of the city. Although still in its infancy it seems destined to become one of LA's main attractions. With everything from Greek sculptures to paintings by European masters and modern photography, the museum is surrounded by ponds, beautiful landscaping and a fine herb garden.

✚ 46A4
Getty Center
✉ 1200 Getty Center Drive
☎ 310/440 7300
🕐 Tue–Thu, Sun 10–6, Fri, Sat 10–9
✋ Free ($7 fee for parking)

GRIFFITH PARK ✪✪✪

Here, in the Santa Monica Mountain range, Griffith Park contains the LA Zoo, Griffith Observatory and Planetarium (closed for renovation until 2006), as well as Travel Town, an outdoor transportation museum. The Observatory is the perfect spot to view the Hollywood sign and the entire city, while the Planetarium features incredible laserium shows. There are horseback riding and children's rides and attractions, plus plenty of picnic areas.

✚ 46B5
✉ Mount Hollywood
☎ 323/664 1191 (Observatory/Planetarium); 323/666 4650 (Zoo); 323/913 4688 (tourist information)
🕐 Hours vary so call for information.
✋ The park is free; some attractions have moderate fees

HOLLYWOOD (▶ 21, TOP TEN)

HOLLYWOOD WAX MUSEUM ✪✪

Over 220 of Hollywood's greatest stars, political leaders and sports greats—all made of wax, but very lifelike—are on show at the Hollywood Wax Museum. Also included are displays on television, motion pictures and religion. Exhibits rotate every six months or so. The Chamber of Horrors is a favorite, as well as the recent additions of current stars.

✚ 46B4
✉ 6767 Hollywood Boulevard
☎ 323/462 8860
🕐 Sun–Thu 10–midnight, Fri–Sat to 1am
✋ Moderate

HUNTINGTON LIBRARY, ART GALLERY AND ✪✪✪
BOTANICAL GARDENS

The historical library contains over four million items, including art treasures and an extraordinary treasury of rare and precious manuscripts. After taking in the Huntington's art and books, take a walk through the immaculate botanical gardens, the best in the state. Here, 15 separate garden areas contain around 14,000 different types of plants and trees. Arrive early because the grounds fill up fast.

🔲 47D5
✉ 1151 Oxford Road, San Marino
☎ 626/405 2141
🕐 Tue–Fri 12–4.30pm, Sat–Sun 10.30–4.30
👆 Moderate

LITTLE TOKYO ✪✪

The city's Japanese quarter features the 40-shop Japanese Village Plaza, which resembles a rural village. Also here are Noguchi Plaza, with its fan-shaped Japan America Theatre, the Japanese American National Museum, and quiet Japanese gardens. Some great sushi bars can also be found here.

🔲 46C4
✉ First Street & Central Avenue

LONG BEACH ✪✪

This rapidly growing city, just south of Los Angeles, is now California's fifth largest city. Its Shoreline Village and Wilmore Park surround the Convention and Entertainment Center, a popular corporate convention spot. Boats to Catalina Island depart from Golden Shore Boulevard.

Of special interest is the *Queen Mary*, which came to rest in Long Beach in 1967. With 12 decks and weighing in at 50,000 tons, it is the largest passenger ship ever built, the *crème de la crème* of 1932 art deco luxury. There are lots of shops and eateries on board.

🔲 46C1
✉ Pier J, Long Beach Harbor
☎ 562/435 3511
🕐 Daily 10–5
👆 Free; moderate-priced guided tours

LOS ANGELES STATE AND ✪✪✪
COUNTY ARBORETUM

The trees and shrubs in the 127-acre (51-ha) splendor of the Los Angeles Arboretum are arranged according to the

🔲 47D5
✉ 301 N Baldwin Avenue, Arcadia
☎ 626/821 3222
🕐 Daily 9–4.30 (extended hours in summer)
👆 Inexpensive; various discounts

The delightful Queen Anne guest house in Los Angeles Arboretum

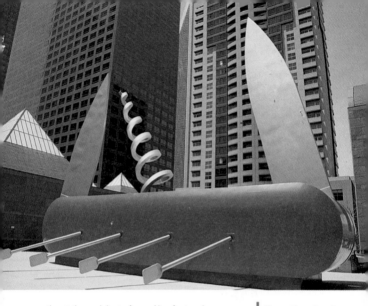

continent they originate from. Also featured are green-houses, a bird sanctuary and historic buildings like the Queen Anne Cottage, home of the estate's former owner, Elia Jackson Baldwin. Picnic areas and tours available.

The cutting edge of contemporary sculpture on display at MOCA

MANN'S CHINESE THEATRE ✪✪✪
Originally Grauman's Chinese Theatre, Mann's, a prime Hollywood tourist attraction, is a good starting point for a tour of Los Angeles (➤ 21). The theater was opened in 1927 by showman Sid Grauman, and whenever a film was premiered here, stars left their hand or foot prints.

➕ 46B4
✉ 6925 Hollywood Boulevard
☎ 323/464 8111

MUSEUM OF CONTEMPORARY ART (MOCA) ✪✪✪
This seven-tiered museum (much of which is below street level) has 11 giant pyramidal skylights and a 53-ft (16-m) barrel-vaulted entrance. It is dedicated to works of art since the 1940s and features traveling exhibitions. Also at Geffen Contemporary and Pacific Design Center.

➕ 46B4
✉ 250 S Grand Avenue
☎ 213/621 2766
🕐 Mon, Fri 11–5, Thu 11–8, Sat, Sun 11–6
✋ Moderate, free Thu

PETERSEN AUTOMOTIVE MUSEUM ✪✪✪
If you are an automotive fan, the Petersen Museum, with one of the largest auto collections in the world, is a must. It explores automotive history and culture from the earliest jalopies. Highlights are the 1957 Ferrari 250 Testa Rossa, and customized cars from Dean Jeffries and George Barris.

➕ 46B4
✉ 6060 Wilshire Boulevard
☎ 323/930 CARS
🕐 Tue–Sun 10–6
✋ Moderate

SOUTHWEST MUSEUM ✪
This mission-revival style building, high above downtown LA, focuses on Native American art, including jewelry, basketwork and weaving. The museum's founder, Charles Lummis, director of the Los Angeles Library in 1907, also donated rare books to the museum.

➕ 46C4
✉ 234 Museum Drive
☎ 323/221 2164
🕐 Tue–Sun 10–5
✋ Moderate

📍 46B5
✉️ 100 Universal City Plaza, Universal City
☎️ 800-UNIVERSAL
🕐 Daily, from 9 or 10am; closing hours vary
✋ Expensive

The beachfront, Venice Beach—haunt of skateboarders and rollerbladers

UNIVERSAL STUDIOS AND CITYWALK ✪✪✪

For a fascinating behind-the-scenes look at movie-making, plan to spend the better part of a day at Universal Studios, the world's biggest and busiest motion picture and television studio-cum-theme park. Citywalk features outdoor dining and a wide variety of shops that are a cut above what you might expect. There are huge outdoor screens that show music videos and movie previews and a theater complex shows all the latest movies.

The upper and lower sections are connected by a long escalator, making the 420-acre (170-ha) park easy to navigate. Some of the more interesting sets still standing are from such films as *The Sting, Animal House* and *Home Alone*. There are theme rides based on other successful films such as *Revenge of the Mummy* and *Jurassic Park*.

📍 46A3
✉️ 15 miles (24km) from downtown Los Angeles, access via Lincoln Boulevard

VENICE BEACH ✪✪

Just south along the beach from Santa Monica is Venice Beach. Although it appears to be a throwback to the 1960s, it is really a thriving enclave for modern bohemians. The neighborhood was founded in 1905 by Abbot Kinney, who hoped to create a haven for artistic types. Gondolas were imported from Italy and, for a time, the canals were eerily similar to those in Europe. Try a free self-guided tour. The most popular today is the Ocean Front Walk, teeming with visitors, street performers and souvenir stands. You can also rent a bicycle or rollerblades.

📍 46C3
✉️ 1765 E 107th Street
☎️ 213/847 4646

WATTS TOWERS ✪✪✪

Italian immigrant Simon Rodia took 30 years to build these extraordinary towers by himself, using scraps of whatever materials he could find. Saved from demolition by local residents, the towers are currently being restored.

A Drive Around Los Angeles

This drive winds through some of LA's most exclusive neighborhoods, then west to Malibu.

From the Hollywood Bowl, drive north, veering to the left on to Cahuenga Boulevard. Drive to the Mulholland Drive turn-off, go left and continue on to Mulholland west.

Along Mulholland are several turn-offs for viewing the city and the San Fernando Valley below.

Continue westward on Mulholland to the 405 Freeway, entering southbound.

Take the first exit (Getty Center Drive), the site of the Getty Center (➤ 51).

Continue south on the 405 to Sunset Boulevard and exit. Turn right on to Sunset and drive westward. Continue to Bundy Drive and turn left at the light. Travel south about a mile (1.6km) to reach the stoplight at San Vincente. Go through the light, turn left and right to continue on Bundy.

Just past the next stop-light is the Simpson-Goldman murder scene, to your right.

Return to Sunset and turn left. Travel west on Sunset through the Pacific Palisades, to Pacific Coast Highway, along the ocean.

At the junction of Sunset and the Pacific Coast Highway is Gladstones 4 Fish, a great place to take lunch.

Continue north on Pacific Coast Highway to Malibu. Las Tunas State Beach is a good beach to spend time on. Continue north to Malibu Canyon Road and turn right at the light. Follow the road over the Santa Monica Mountains and turn into Las Virgines Road. Continue to the on-ramp to the 101 Freeway, and follow it south to the Highland exit and the Hollywood Bowl.

Distance
60 miles (97km)

Time
About 5 hours

Start/end point
Hollywood Bowl
➕ 46B4

Lunch
Gladstones 4 Fish ($$)
✉ 17300 Pacific Coast Highway, Pacific Palisades
☎ 310/454 3474

Hollywood landmark: Entrance to Paramount Studios

San Diego

The beautiful Mission Bay and world-famous San Diego Zoo are highlights of this city, one of the most laid-back areas in the US.

For excitement, there's Sea World or the San Diego Wild Animal Park. For serenity, the Japanese Friendship Garden's traditional sand-and-stone garden and wooded canyon view is the perfect picnic spot. Those interested in science will appreciate The Reuben H. Fleet Space Theater and Science Center. Its Space Theater's OMNIMAX films bring outer space up close, while the Aerospace Museum showcases heroes of aviation and space.

Old Town commemorates the first permanent settlement in California and still has many of the city's original buildings. Trolley tours through the six-block area make seeing the sights easy.

"Wouldn't it be wonderful to have a zoo in San Diego? I believe I'll build one."

DR. HENRY WEGEFORTH,
on hearing the roar of caged lions at
the California Panama
Exposition (1906)

———————●———————

The modern San Diego skyline

San Diego

San Diego rarely gets rain, never freezes, has an average annual daytime temperature between 58 and 70°F (15–21°C), and more than 70 miles (113km) of sandy beaches. California's second largest city, it retains a small-town ambience. Ralph Waldo Emerson must have visited San Diego when he said "California has better days and more of them."

The lighthouse at Cabrillo National Monument

What to See in San Diego

BALBOA PARK (► 16, TOP TEN)

🔳 59A2

THE BEACHES ✪✪✪
The most popular of the city's beaches is Pacific Beach (known as "PB" by the locals), which features The Tourmaline Surfing Park, a surfer's paradise. Mission Beach has a 3-mile (5-km) walk of shops and skateboard, rollerblade and bicycle rental stands. Ocean Beach is one of the liveliest in San Diego, and a good place to fish. Point Loma is an upscale beach, with spectacular views of the naval ships' comings and goings.

🔳 59A1
✉ 10 miles (16km) west of I-8 on Catalina Boulevard
☎ 619/557 5450
🕐 Daily 9–5.15
💵 Inexpensive

CABRILLO NATIONAL MONUMENT ✪✪
A 144-acre (58-ha) park along steep cliffs, Cabrillo rewards with great views of San Diego Bay, and it's an especially good place to spot gray whales migrating to Mexico between mid-December and mid-March. The Old Point Loma Lighthouse, dating from 1855, is 25 miles (43km) out to sea, but visible from here on a clear day.

🔳 59B1
✉ Visitor Center at 1100 Orange Avenue
☎ 619/236 1212

CORONADO ISLAND ✪✪✪
A combination of wealthy enclave and naval base, Coronado sits just across the bay from downtown San Diego. The easiest way to reach it is on the Bay Ferry.

Scripps Oceanography and Birch Aquarium
Point La Jolla
La Jolla Caves
LA JOLLA
La Jolla Museum of Contemporary Art
Soledad Natural Park
UNIVERSITY CITY
Los Angeles
Miramar Naval Air Station
SAN DIEGO
San Diego Wild Animal Park
San Clemente Canyon
NORTH CLAIREMONT
TIERRASANTA
3
0   5 km
PACIFIC BEACH
CLAIREMONT
Tecolote Canyon Natural Park
Montgomery Field
SERRA MESA
San Diego Stadium
GRANTVILLE
Mission San Diego de Alcala
MISSION BEACH
Mission Bay Park
LINDA VISTA
University of San Diego
Alvarado Canyon
Aztec Bowl
Sea World
Mission Valley
2
OCEAN BEACH
Sports Arena
Old Town State Historic Park
Presidio Park
SAN DIEGO
Chollas Park
MIDWAY
San Diego Int Airport
Balboa Park
San Diego Zoo
Museums
Sunset Cliffs Park
POINT LOMA
Maritime Museum
Gaslamp Quarter
ENCANTO
Seaport Village
North Island US Naval Air Station
Embarcadero
1
Cabrillo National Monument
CORONADO
CORONADO BAY BRIDGE
San Diego Bay
NATIONAL CITY
LINCOLN ACRES
Tijuana, Mexico
A   B   C

Leaving from Broadway Pier downtown, the ferry arrives at Old Ferry Landing in Coronado in 15 minutes. You can also reach the island via the towering San Diego–Coronado Bay Bridge (toll). The main attraction on the island is Hotel Del Coronado (➤ 102). A testament to the beauty of Victorian architecture, the "Del" was opened in 1888, and film buffs might remember it as one of the main locations

☎ 619/437 8788 (Visitor Center), 619/234 4111 (Bay Ferry information)
▥ Inexpensive

The Victorian-style Hotel del Coronado

GASLAMP QUARTER (➤ 62)

HOUSE OF PACIFIC RELATIONS   ✪✪

The culture and art of 31 nations is housed in the museum's 15 California/Spanish-style cottages located in the Pan American Plaza. Other Plaza attractions are the Aerospace Museum, San Diego Automotive Museum and the open-air Starlight Bowl.

✚ 59B1
✉ Balboa Park
☎ 619/234 0739
🕐 Sun, 2nd and 4th Tue of month
🎟 Free; donations welcome

LA JOLLA   ✪✪✪

Pronounced *La Hoya* (Spanish for "The Jewel") this picturesque cove must surely be one of the prettiest places in the whole state. Just north of San Diego proper, it is considered the best place to examine marine life in a wild environment. This unspoiled piece of coastline offers expensive restaurants and boutiques on its two main thoroughfares: Prospect Street and Girard Avenue. Just north of La Jolla are the equally scenic towns of Del Mar and Solana Beach. Relatively undiscovered by tourists, these beaches epitomize the beauty and tranquillity of Southern California.

✚ 59A3
✉ 10 miles (16km) north of San Diego via I 805 or Highway 1

The crystal clear waters at La Jolla

MARITIME MUSEUM OF SAN DIEGO   ✪✪✪

Basically just three ships are moored on the Embarcadero but oh, what legendary ships they are! The pick of the bunch is the 1863 *Star of India*, a fully equipped three-mast sailing ship, the oldest iron-hulled ship in America still afloat. San Francisco's *Berkeley* was the ferry used to evacuate victims of the 1906 earthquake. The 1904 steam-powered yacht *Medea* still occasionally sails around the Bay.

✚ 59B1
✉ 1306 North Harbor Drive
☎ 619/234 9153
🕐 Daily 9–8 (closes 9 in summer)
🎟 Moderate

Mission San Diego de Alcala was Serra's first mission in California

MISSION BAY PARK ✪✪

There are miles of cycling paths throughout this huge aquatic park, and a bicycle rental stand can be found just off East Mission Bay Drive. Kite flying and volleyball are popular pastimes here, and just about anything to do with the water, as well as golf, picnicking and camping, can be found. The park is also the home of Sea World (▶ 64), and for many families the main reason for coming here. Just next to the park is Fiesta Island, popular with the locals for jet skiing and the curious game of "over the line" baseball.

 59A2
🕐 Daily
💲 Free
ℹ 2688 E Mission Bay Drive
   ☎ 619/276 8200

MUSEUM OF MAN ✪✪

The San Diego Museum of Man, located below the California Tower, offers eclectic, ever-changing exhibits from Californians and Hopi tribes, ancient Egypt and mummies, to Mayas and early man (▶ 16).

➕ 59B1
✉ Balboa Park
☎ 619/239 2001
🕐 Daily 10–4.30
💲 Inexpensive

OLD TOWN SAN DIEGO STATE HISTORIC PARK ✪✪✪

The remains of the first European settlement in California, Old Town is preserved with National Park status. The most important area of Old Town is the Mission San Diego de Alcala, California's first mission, founded in 1769 by Father Junípero Serra. Restored and still used for services, it has beautiful gardens and adobe structures and houses the Museum de Luis Jayme. One of the oldest buildings, Casa de Estudillo, has survived several hundred years.

Old Town Plaza was a general meeting place and center for festivals, religious celebrations and even bullfights in the mid-1800s. Here you'll find the visitors' center where you can sign up for free tours of the grounds.

➕ 59B2
✉ San Diego Avenue, at Twiggs Street
☎ 619/220 5422
🕐 Daily 10–5, closed Jan 1, Thanksgiving, Christmas Day
💲 Free

A Walk Around San Diego

Distance
3.5 miles (5.5km)

Time
3 hours

Start point
Visitors' Center, Old Town
State Historic Park
🚩 59B2

End point
Old Town Plaza
🚩 59B2

Lunch
Casa de Bandini ($)
✉ 2754 Calhoun Street
☎ 619/297 8211
🕐 Sun–Thu 11–9, Fri–Sat
11–9.30

Starting at the Old Town visitors' center, you pass historic buildings, museums and sites that encompass the oldest and most beautiful part of San Diego.

From the visitors' center, walk southward and turn east on San Diego Avenue, continuing to the Machado–Silvas Adobe house.

This is one of the more famous buildings built in the mid-19th century, and houses the Courthouse and the Colorado House/Wells Fargo Museum.

After touring the house, continue a short distance north to Mason Street.

Here you will see the Mason Street School. Built in 1865, this one-room building was San Diego's first publicly owned school.

Go north on Mason to San Diego Avenue, then turn east to Dodson's Corner.

Dodson's Corner is a group of false-front shops where merchants sometimes dress in period costume. Across San Diego Avenue is the San Diego Union Museum, home of the state's longest running newspaper.

From here go north on Twiggs Street to Calhoun Street.

At Calhoun you will see the Steelly Stables, and Blackhawk Smith and Stable, both worth a look.

Walk west on Calhoun to the Alvarado House and Johnson House, two beautiful and historic structures. Retrace your steps back to Mason Street, then head south to visit the Casa De Estudillo. After touring the Casa, step across the street back into Old Town Plaza to end your tour.

Street art in the Gaslamp Quarter

To complement your stroll through Old Town, you could visit the nearby Gaslamp Quarter, bound by Broadway, 4th, 6th and Harbor streets, which gives a comprehensive history of San Diego's architecture.

PRESIDIO PARK ✪✪
Formerly the fort here protected Mission San Diego de Alcala. The park is up the hill from the center of Old Town. As you sit on the benches scattered among the trees of this 50-acre (20-ha) park you will have wonderful views of the Old Town expanse. San Diego's landmark museum, the Junipero Serra, sits high atop the hill where California's first mission and presidio were founded. Spanish, Mexican and Native American aspects of San Diego's history are recalled with exhibits of furniture, clothing, household items and other artifacts of the past 200 years.

➕ 59B2
✉ 2727 Presidio Drive
☎ 619/297 3258
⏱ Park daily; Junipero Serra Museum daily 10–4.30
♿ Moderate

Rhinos at San Diego Wild Animal Park, Escondido

SAN DIEGO WILD ANIMAL PARK ✪✪
The park, 30 miles (48km) northeast of San Diego, is known for its authentic re-creation of African and Asian terrain. Almost 2,500 endangered animals are presented here by the Zoological Society of San Diego. This 2,100-acre (850-ha) preserve features a monorail tour, Nairobi Village animal shows, hiking trails and botanical exhibits.

➕ 69E1
✉ Via Rancho Pkwy exit off I–15
☎ 619/234 6541
⏱ Daily 9–4
♿ Expensive (combination pass with San Diego Zoo)

SCRIPPS OCEANOGRAPHY AND ✪✪
BIRCH AQUARIUM
Part of the University of California at San Diego, Birch Aquarium and the Memorial Pier are landmarks of the La Jolla coast. Marine scientists have been working here since the turn of the century. The Institute displays the aquatic world in indoor tanks, an on-shore tidepool and through additional oceanographic exhibits showing the latest advances in oceanography.

➕ 59A3
✉ 2300 Expedition Way
☎ 858/534 3474
⏱ Daily 9–5
♿ Moderate

63

www.seaworld.com

59B2

Sea World Drive off the I–5, Mission Bay Park

619/226 3901;

Daily from 10am, closing times vary with season

Expensive

SEA WORLD ✪✪✪

Perhaps one of, if not *the* finest marine biology park in the world, Sea World is impressive, and you can and should plan on spending the better part of a day here. Comfortably spread out over 150 acres (61ha), it features continuous killer whale and dolphin shows, and highly informative marine life exhibits. Between shows, you can touch or view live animals in the petting pools. Also not to miss are the nautical theme playground, marina and state-of-the-art research laboratories.

Sea World is home to killer whales Shamu and Baby Shamu, the real stars of the park, as well as seals, sea lions and walruses. The Rocky Point Preserve is a habitat for dolphins and sea otters, while "Penguin Encounter" has over 300 penguins. Other exhibits include "Pets Rule!" and "Fools with Tools." A family-oriented theme park features interactive games and adventures. Guided tours are available, and in the summer there are evening aquatic shows. Owing to the park's popularity, you can expect long waits for some shows and exhibits, especially during the summer.

Don't forget the re-entry stamp should you decide to leave the park and return later. Ticket sales stop 90 minutes before closing, which is around sunset most of the year, but up until 11pm in the summer.

Sea World deserves a whole day to do it justice

A Drive From San Diego

This drive includes historic Route 1, the Palomar Observatory and the San Diego Wild Animal Park.

Leave downtown on Route 1, going north out of the city. Pass through La Jolla.

Stop to enjoy the view from the cliffs (➤ 60). Also recommended is a stop at Torrey Pines State Preserve, a 1,000-acre (405-ha) area which has one of the world's two surviving stands of the Torrey pine tree. The walking trails are unique and offer a pleasant break from driving.

Continue north through Del Mar (stop at the famous racetrack if you are here in the summer), and on to Solana Beach, and finally Carlsbad.

Carlsbad is one of many pleasant communities in Southern California and is a good place to stop for lunch and do some shopping.

Highway 1 now becomes Interstate 5, which you follow north to SR 78. Exit and proceed east on SR 78 through San Marcos and into Escondido.

Champagne Boulevard in Escondido (🕐 10–5) is the world's only combined winery and car museum, with over 100 American convertibles on display.

From Escondido take SR 17 east to the San Diego Wild Animal Park (➤ 63). Spend a few hours here before continuing on SR 17 to Ramona. At Ramona take the junction on to Highway 67, a beautiful route that takes you past the Barona Indian Reservation. It then becomes the 8 Freeway, returning to downtown San Diego.

Distance
60 miles (97km)

Time
About 5–7 hours, depending on time spent at attractions

Start/end point
Downtown San Diego
✚ 59A3

Lunch
Coyote Bar and Grill ($)
✉ 300 Carlsbad Village Drive
☎ 760/729 4695
🕐 Sun–Thu 11-10, Fri–Sat 11–11

A fine photo opportunity at San Diego Wildlife Park

Rest of California

With its diverse environments and cultures, and its progressive way of thinking, California is more like an independent country than a state. As unique and varied as the major cities are, the outlying regions are even more so. There are the sprawling green vineyards of Napa and Sonoma valleys, the giant trees of Yosemite, Redwood and Sequoia national parks, mountains, deserts, inland seas and, of course, the ocean. The communities themselves range from upscale urban centers like Palm Springs to unpretentious farming and manufacturing towns. The 21 mission communities are perhaps the most charming of all. Their distinctive architectural style features stone and adobe, with whitewashed mud plaster inside and out. The pitched roofs of hewn timber, covered with red tiles, bring elegance and historical import to the entire state.

> *"... wonderful, wonderful, sublime, indescribable, incomprehensible; I never saw anything so truly and appallingly grand; it pays me a hundred times over for visiting California."*
>
> P. T. BARNUM
> after his first visit to California

———————•———————

View from the Sky Jump at Knotts Berry Farm, Anaheim

What to See in the Rest of California

ANAHEIM

Anaheim was originally founded as the center of a wine-producing colony by German immigrants in 1857. The vineyards were replaced by orange groves late in the 19th century, after an especially brutal drought. Oranges thrived until the 1950s, when commercial interests and the rapid growth of the Los Angeles metropolitan area took over. The two main attractions in the area are Disneyland Park (► 18) and Knott's Berry Farm (► 78).

69D1
✉ 46 miles (74km) from Los Angeles via I–5; directly across from Disneyland

BAKERSFIELD

Bakersfield is California's main oil-producing center. Many consider it a less-than-desirable part of California, its furnace-like, 100°F-plus summers a major drawback. However, the downtown area is a vital mix of restored buildings and newer offices. Of note in the town are a genuine schoolhouse, church and a fully restored 1868 log cabin.

The **California Living Museum** focuses on the state's wildlife and native plants, many of which have become rare or endangered.

Kern County Museum has exhibits representing both human and natural history of the area.

69D2
California Living Museum
✉ 10500 Alfred Harrell Highway
☎ 661/872 2256
🕐 Tue–Sun 9–5
🍴 Picnic facilities
💲 Inexpensive

Kern County Museum
✉ 3801 Chester Avenue
☎ 661/852 5000
🕐 Mon–Sat 10–5, Sun noon–5
💲 Moderate

BARSTOW

Barstow is the halfway point between Los Angeles and Las Vegas. Settled in the early 19th century, silver mines flourished in the surrounding areas. The town of **Calico** boomed in the late 1800s, and its mines produced $15 million worth of ore. When the price of silver dropped, the town went bust. Today, you can visit the "ghost town" of Calico to pan for gold, ride the steam railway or see a show at the Calikage Playhouse.

North of Barstow is **Rainbow Basin National Natural Landmark**, formed by the deposit of sediment over millions of years. Fossils, the forces of nature and an abundance of minerals give it its dramatic shapes and colors.

69E2
Calico Ghost Town
✉ 11 miles (18km) northeast of Barstow via I-15
☎ 760/254 2122
🕐 Daily 9–5
🍴 Restaurants moderate
💲 Moderate

Rainbow Basin National Natural Landmark
✉ Fossil Bed Road, 8 miles (13km) north of Barstow via SR 58

BIG BEAR LAKE

One of California's largest recreation areas, the Big Bear Lake region has two distinct sections; Big Bear Lake and Big Bear City, on the eastern end of the lake. Big Bear Village, centered around the lake, is popular for lodging, dining and shopping. Camping, hiking and horse-back riding are available in summer and skiing in winter.

69E2
✉ Big Bear Chamber of Commerce, 630 Bartlett Road
☎ 909/866 4607
🍴 Many restaurants ($–$$$)

CARMEL ✪✪✪

Carmel was established in the late 19th century and has since gained its reputation as a bohemian retreat. It has

some of the most picturesque coastal residences in the state, many in Spanish-Mission style. **Mission San Carlos Borromeo del Rio Carmelo** (1769) was moved to its riverside site here in Carmel in 1771. Father Junípero Serra is buried in the church, which was given the status of minor basilica by the Pope in 1960.

CATALINA ISLAND (▶ 16, TOP TEN)

DEATH VALLEY NATIONAL PARK ✪✪✪

Three million years ago, inner-earth forces tormented, twisted and shook the land in what is now Death Valley, creating snowcapped mountains and superheated valleys. Lakes, formed during the Ice Age, evaporated, leaving alternating layers of mud and salt deposits.

More than three million acres in size, Death Valley ranges in elevation from 282ft (86m) below sea level to slightly over 11,000ft (3,354m) above. Temperatures reach well over 100°F (38°C) in summer, making it one of the hottest regions in the world. **Scotty's Castle**, on the northern boundary of the park, is a Spanish/Moorish construction built by Chicago insurance tycoon Albert Johnson for Walter E. Scott, alias "Death Valley Scotty."

✚ 68B3

Mission San Carlos Borromeo del Rio Carmelo
✉ 3080 Rio Road
☎ 831/624 1271
🕐 Mon–Fri 9.30–4.30, Sat, Sun 10–30–4.30
💰 Free, but donations accepted

Left: *Mission San Carlos Borromeo del Rio Carmelo, final resting place of Junípero Serra*
Below: *Bicycling at Big Bear Lake*

✚ 69E3
✉ Furnace Creek Visitors Center
☎ 760/786 3244
🕐 Daily 8–5
♿ Some areas disabled accessible
💰 Inexpensive
❓ Camping facilities

Scotty's Castle
☎ 760/786 2392
🕐 Daily 8.30–5.30
💰 Moderate

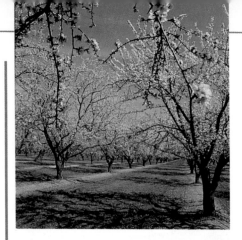

The beautiful Blossom Trail in the fruit orchards around Fresno

➕ 68B5
Clarke Memorial Museum
🗺 Third and "E" streets
☎ 707/443 1947
🕐 Tue–Sat 11–4
🎟 Free

Blue Ox Millworks
🗺 Foot of "X" street
☎ 707/444 3437
🕐 Mon–Fri 9–5, Sat by appointment
🎟 Inexpensive

Sequoia Park
🗺 Glatt and "W" Streets
☎ 707/442 6552
🕐 Daily 10am–dusk
🍴 Picnic facilities
🎟 Inexpensive

➕ 68C3
Metropolitan Museum of Art, History and Science
🗺 1555 Van Ness Avenue
☎ 559/441 1444
🕐 Tue–Sun 11–5
🎟 Inexpensive

➕ 68C4
Angel's Camp Museum
🗺 753 South Main Street
☎ 209/736 2963
🕐 Mar–end Dec daily 10–3; Jan–end Feb Sat, Sun 10–3
🎟 Inexpensive

EUREKA ✪✪
Eureka is the largest town on California's northernmost coast. Set along Humboldt Bay, it is home to an impressive fishing fleet. Its name, from the Greek word for "I have found it," refers to the cries from many gold miners (called '49ers) in the 19th century. The Old Town section is worth a visit for its elegantly refurbished Victorian homes.

The old 1912 building, once the town's main bank, now houses the **Clarke Memorial Museum**. It houses an excellent collection of California Native American historic artifacts.

Blue Ox Millworks is a working mill that includes a blacksmith shop and a re-creation of a logging camp. **Sequoia Park,** a beautiful grove of virgin redwoods in 52 acres (21ha), has a formal flower garden, duck pond, and deer and elk paddocks.

FRESNO ✪✪
Fresno lies in the heart of the San Joaquin Valley. One of the foremost agricultural areas in the country, it is also the gateway to the Sierra Nevada's three national parks.

The town's fine **Metropolitan Museum of Art, History and Science** features an extensive collection of Asian art, as well as American still-life paintings. Wild Water Adventure Park, on E Shaw Avenue, contains over 20 water rides, pools and a small fishing lake.

GOLD COUNTRY TOWNS ✪✪✪
Also known as the Mother Lode Country, this scenic area extends 300 miles (484km) along Highway 49, through the western Sierra Nevada foothills. Once the thriving Old West, it is now mostly ghost towns, several of which are open to tourists.

Angel's Camp Museum, in Angel's Camp (➤ 74), was the center for gravel and quartz mining in 1849. You can see photographs, relics and 3 acres (1.2ha) of old mining equipment from the old days.

Marshall Gold Discovery State Historic Park is where James Marshall discovered gold. The drive-through park features a replica of Sutter's Mill and memorial statue and grave site of James Marshall.

The Empire Mine State Historic Park (➤ 74), 2 miles (3.5km) east of Grass Valley, is the Gold Country's best preserved quartz mining operation. During the boom years, the 367 miles (592km) of mine shafts produced six million ounces of gold.

Mercer Caverns, 1 mile (1.6km) north of Murphys, via Main Street, were discovered in 1885 by Walter Mercer, a gold prospector. The 45-minute tour gives the opportunity to view the enormous stalagmites and stalactites close up.

JOSHUA TREE NATIONAL MONUMENT ✪✪✪
Known for its distinctive Joshua trees (a desert tree of the yucca species), and its uniquely shaped rock formations, the park connects the "high" and "low" deserts. In the park is Key's View, a high elevation with incredible views on a clear day. Not to be missed is the Cholla Cactus Garden, about 10 miles (16km) south of the Oasis Visitors Center.

> ### Did you know ?
> UFO devotees insist there is a secret starship base hidden somewhere in the brush-dotted hills of the park at Joshua Tree. At Giant Rock Airport (2477 Belfield, off Reches Road and Highway 247, Yucca Valley) you can visit a mysterious 40-ft (12-m) dome, Integration, a showpiece for UFO cultists.

Marshall Gold Discovery State Historic Park
- ✉ North fork of the American River and Highway 49, Coloma
- ☎ 530/622 3470
- 🕐 Museum daily 10–3; park 8–sunset
- 💰 Inexpensive

➕ 69E1
- ✉ Oasis Vistors Center, National Monument Drive, 29 Palms
- ☎ 760/367 5500
- 🕐 Daily 8–5
- 💰 Inexpensive

The striking Joshua tree is said to be so named because Western pioneers believed it resembled the biblical Joshua raising his arms to the heavens and stopping the sun so the Israelites could win their battle

A Drive Through the Gold Country

This drive will take you through Gold Country along historic Highway 49.

Begin in Mariposa, where SR 49 meets SR 140.

Here you can visit the California State Mining and Mineral Museum and the Mariposa County Museum.

Proceed north on SR 49 to Chinese Camp and the State Historic Park. A few miles north is Jamestown.

Gold was discovered in Jamestown in 1848

Jamestown served as a backdrop for the film *High Noon* and the television series *Little House on the Prairie*.

Follow 49 north, stopping in Tuttletown.

You can view a replica of Mark Twain's cabin on Jackass Hill (Tuttletown was originally called Jackass Gulch).

Continue to Columbia.

Here you can try your hand at panning for gold, or ride an authentic stagecoach.

Continue north on 49 to Angel's Camp.

This is where Mark Twain first heard the "jumping frog" story from bartender Ben Coon. If you are here in May, don't miss the frog jumping contest. The foundation of Angel's Mine, one of the region's most profitable, can be found across from the Catholic Church.

Continue north to Jackson and Placerville.

Jackson was once home of the Mohawk Indians, and Placerville was formerly known as "Hangtown." Gold Bug Mine is worth a visit.

Further north are Coloma, Auburn and Grass Valley.

The latter is home to Empire Mine State Historic Park (► 73) and North Star Mine Museum, both offering tours.

The drive ends in Nevada City.

Distance
Approximately 100 miles (161km)

Time
8 hours

Start point
Mariposa
✚ 68C3

End point
Nevada City
✚ 68C4

Lunch
National Hotel Restaurant ($)
✉ 18183 Main Street, Jamestown
☎ 209/984 3446

LAKE ARROWHEAD ⭐⭐

Known locally as a sophisticated mountain getaway, this is where LA's wealthy spend leisurely weekends in luxury homes. Restrictive development laws help preserve the area's natural beauty. Swimming and boating are popular activities in summer, and skiing in winter.

➕ 69E2
✉ Chamber of Commerce, Lake Arrowhead Village
☎ 909/337 3715
🕐 Mon–Fri 9–5, Sat 10–3

LAKE TAHOE ⭐⭐⭐

Situated on the California–Nevada stateline, Lake Tahoe is one of the most popular resort communities in the state. Although this beautiful lake is 6,228ft (1,899m) above sea level, it never freezes because of its depth. You will find top-notch ski areas here, and in summer, water sports include lake cruises, water skiing and sailing.

For a spectacular aerial view of the entire area, including the site of the 1960 Winter Olympic Games, ride the gondola to the top of the Squaw Valley Ski Area.

➕ 68C4
Squaw Valley Cable Car
✉ 1960 Squaw Valley Road, Olympic Valley
☎ 530/583 6985
🕐 Call to check. Closed mid Oct–Dec 1
✋ Moderate

Bumpass Hell, at Lassen

LASSEN VOLCANIC NATIONAL PARK ⭐⭐⭐

Lassen Park stretches over 100,000 acres (40,486ha) in the northeastern corner of California, where the Cascade and Sierra Nevada mountains meet. Highlights are Lassen Peak, Cinder Cone, Prospect Peak and Mount Harkness, the latter two volcanoes topped by cinder cones.

Lassen's numerous volcanic eruptions subsided in 1921 and have been replaced by inviting hot springs and lakes, lava flows and mudpots, all linked together by hiking trails that lead to the summit and back.

➕ 68C5
✉ 9 miles (15km) east of Mineral, via SR 36
☎ 530/595 4444
🕐 Year-round

MAMMOTH LAKES RECREATION AREA ⭐⭐

This giant popular resort area in the Inyo National Forest has world-class skiing, and in summertime it's a mountain biking mecca. There is also good camping, fishing and horseback riding here. Hike to the 101-ft (31-m) Rainbow Falls, or visit the Devil's Postpile National Monument, 60-ft (18-m) multi-sided columns that are by-products of former volcanic activity.

➕ 69D3
✉ Chamber of Commerce, PO Box 123, Mammoth Lakes, 93546
☎ 760/934 3068
🕐 Mon–Fri 9–5
🍴 Restaurants ($$)

Mendocino Chamber of Commerce
🔲 68A5
✉ 332 North Main Street
☎ 707/961 6300
🕐 Daily 11–4

Mendocino Art Center
✉ 45200 Little Lake Street
☎ 707/937 5818 or 800/653 3328
🕐 Call for times
🖐 Moderate

🔲 68C4

McHenry Museum & Mansion
✉ 1402 "I" Street
☎ 209/577 5366 (museum); 577 5341 (mansion)
🕐 Tue–Sun noon–4. Closed major holidays
🖐 Free, donations requested
❓ Tours of mansion offered Sun–Thu 1–4, Fri noon–3

🔲 68C2
✉ 845 Embarcadero Road, Suite D
☎ 805/772 4467
🕐 Mon–Fri 8.30–5, Sat 10–4
🖐 Free

Museum of Natural History
✉ Morro Bay State Park
☎ 805/772 2694
🕐 Daily 10–5
🖐 Inexpensive

Tiger's Folly Cruises
✉ 1205 Embarcadero
☎ 805/772 2257
🕐 Call for schedules
🖐 Inexpensive

MENDOCINO

Mendocino, off scenic US 1, is perhaps the most charming small town in California. It is noted for its Cape Cod and Victorian-style architecture and its active, artistic community. The entire town is on the National Register of Historic Places. Film buffs will recognize it from such films as *The Summer of '42, East of Eden* and television's *Murder She Wrote*.

The **Art Center** is the epicenter of the many art museums in the community, and includes galleries, live theater and arts and craft fairs.

MODESTO

This quintessential California town was made famous by George Lucas's film *American Graffiti*. Near the center of the state, it is the home of the Blue Diamond Almonds company.

The **McHenry Museum** re-creates a 19th-century school, blacksmith shop, kitchen, country store and others with changing exhibits. The **McHenry Mansion**, a block away, exhibits antique furnishings and artwork in a restored Victorian home.

MONTEREY PENINSULA (➤ 22, TOP TEN)

MORRO BAY

Morro Rock, the conical, volcano-shaped rock that towers 578ft (176m) out of the Pacific Ocean, sits guarding the entrance to Morro Bay, which is known primarily for its commercial fishing and oyster farming. Although the town has a modest tourist trade, the locals are mostly concerned with the daily business of fishing. Beneath the rock stretches a 5-mile (8-km) long beach with 85-ft (26-m) high white sand dunes that serve as a habitat for bird and plant life.

The Morro Bay Arts Festival takes place each weekend in October, and the **Museum of Natural History** exhibits marine life native to the central coast, including the Bay's sea lions. **Tiger's Folly Cruises** offers harbor cruises.

The State Park, south of Morro Bay, is beautiful and a must for those who enjoy camping and hiking. The campgrounds are at the southern end of the park surrounded by cypress and eucalyptus.

The Galley Restaurant serves delicious seafood meals.

MOUNT PALOMAR ✪✪✪

Palomar Observatory houses the world-famous 200-in (513-cm) Hale telescope. High above the distracting, bright city lights, the observatory also has several smaller telescopes, used to monitor the planet's movement. The small Greenway Museum contains photographs of the observatory's celestial sightings.

✚ 69E1
✉ 4.5 miles (7km) north of San Diego on SR 6
☎ 626/395 4033
🕐 Daily 9–4
💷 Free

MOUNT SHASTA ✪✪

Spiritual-minded Californians flock to this mountain because it is said to be a "vortex of spiritual energy." For the more earthbound there is hiking, climbing, and skiing in winter. Several surrounding lakes offer waterside camping, fishing and watersports, including skating in winter.

The **Mount Shasta State Fish Hatchery**, in the center of the area, produces 5 to 10 million trout annually to stock Northern California lakes.

✚ 68B6
✉ Chamber of Commerce Visitors Bureau, 300 Pine Street
☎ 800/926 4865

Mount Shasta State Fish Hatchery
☎ 530/926 2215
🕐 Daily 7am–dusk
💷 Free

OAKLAND ✪✪

Linked to San Francisco by the Bay Bridge, Oakland has long suffered from its close proximity to the city across the bay. In reality, it is a culturally rich and diversified town and has counted among its famous citizens Jack London and Gertrude Stein. **Oakland Museum** has an extensive collection of historical and contemporary art housed in the Gallery of California Art. The museum is one of the best in the state for studying the diverse cultural make-up and subsequent historical progress.

Lake Merritt, created in the late 19th century by the damming of a section of the Oakland estuary, was one of the first natural wildlife preserves established in the US.

✚ 68B4

Oakland Museum
✉ 11th and Oak Street
☎ 510/238 2200
🕐 Wed–Sat 10–5, Sun noon–5
💷 Inexpensive

Mount Shasta is usually snow-capped all year

Orange County

Known by Californians as the "conservative" enclave of the state, Orange County is a sprawling, seemingly endless expanse of humanity between Los Angeles and San Diego, with its own unique charms.

DISNEYLAND PARK (▶ 18, TOP TEN)

FESTIVAL OF THE ARTS/PAGEANT OF THE MASTERS ✪✪

A state-of-the-art art exhibit in the scenic wooded Laguna Canyon, this is a landmark event, the former featuring an exhibit of 150 Laguna artists of all kinds. The most interesting aspect of this seven-week event, however, is the Pageant of the Masters, in which human models stand perfectly still for three minutes in re-creations of famous paintings and sculptures, with a musical accompaniment.

Off map 47E1
Laguna Canyon Road, Laguna Beach
949/494 1145
Jul–end Aug 10am–11pm
Expensive

HUNTINGTON ART CENTER ✪

Though small, the Huntington Art Center is concerned with local contemporary art and architecture in a big way. It has been renovated and is a favorite with many local artists. Films are shown the first and third Friday of each month.

47D1
538 Main Street E, Huntington Beach
714/374 1650
Wed–Sun noon–6, Sun noon–4
Free

INTERNATIONAL SURFING MUSEUM ✪✪

Huntington Beach calls itself "Surf City," with good reason, and is a mecca for surfing enthusiasts. Exhibits tell the sport's history, and the store sells surf gear, all, of course, to the music of the Beach Boys.

47D1
Olive Street
714/960 3483
Summer daily noon–5; winter Thu–Mon noon–5
Inexpensive

KNOTT'S BERRY FARM ✪✪✪

One of California's original theme parks, Knott's has grown from a true berry farm to a modern 150-acre (61-ha) attraction with over 165 rides. The Western theme areas include Ghost Town and Gold Mine Ride. Other attractions include Camp Snoopy, Wild Water Wilderness, Mystery Lodge, Reflection Lake, California Marketplace and Kingdom of the Dinosaurs. For the adventurous, there are four awesome rollercoasters, the Boomerang, Montezooma's Revenge, the Jaguar and the Silver Bullet. And, finally, for the truly hungry, Knott's serves its original, delicious, world-famous boysenberry pie.

47E2
8039 Beach Boulevard, Buena Park
714/220 5200
Subject to change; call for current times
Expensive

LAGUNA ART MUSEUM ✪✪✪

The Laguna Art Museum was founded in 1918 and is the showcase venue for the Laguna Art Association. It usually features several visiting exhibits of paintings and sculpture by California artists. On permanent display are historical California landscapes and vintage photographs of the region.

Off map 47E1
Pacific Coast Highway and Cliff Drive, Laguna Beach
949/494 8971
Daily 11–5 Moderate

MISSION SAN JUAN CAPISTRANO ✪✪✪

Founded in 1776, this is one of California's most beautiful missions, and the only building still standing where Father Serra said mass. On 19 March each year, the Feast of St. Joseph celebrates the legendary "return of the swallows."

🔹 69D1
✉ Cnr of Ortega Highway/ Camino Capistrano
☎ 949/234 1300
🕐 Daily 8:30–5

Did you know ?

*The swallows of San Juan Capistrano have the reputation of returning every March 19.
In reality, they return over a period of several weeks.
They leave their winter home in South America around October 23 on their 6,000-mile (9,677-km) flight home to spend spring and summer in Southern California.*

Mission San Juan Capistrano, the seventh of the California missions

SHERMAN LIBRARY AND GARDENS ✪✪

The unique gardens here are filled with orchids and koi ponds, while the library itself is a large building, taking up a whole city block. It functions as a center of historical research for the region. There is an extensive collection of historical Orange County documents and photographs.

🔹 Off map 47E1
✉ 2647 E Coast Highway, Newport Beach
☎ 949/673 2261
🕐 Gardens daily 10.30–4
🖐 Inexpensive

YORBA LINDA ✪✪

The Richard Nixon Presidential Library and Birthplace, in Yorba Linda, has galleries, theaters and gardens, and personal memorabilia of this former US president. The grounds feature the small house where he was born, his post-presidency private study and a re-creation of the White House's Lincoln Sitting Room.

🔹 47F2
✉ 18001 Yorba Linda Boulevard
☎ 714/993 3393
🕐 Mon–Sat 10–5, Sun 11–5.
🖐 Moderate

In the Know

10
Ways to Be a Local

Dress casual but trendy. Sunwear and exercise clothes in the south; alternative wear in San Francisco; hiking boots and jeans in the north.

Carry a cellular phone and/or handheld device.

In Los Angeles, talk about movie deals.

In San Francisco, talk about the fog.

In San Diego and the desert areas, don't talk, just smile in a laid-back manner.

Absolutely no one walks in Los Angeles, so rent a convertible, or better still, a Mercedes convertible.

Eat light and healthy meals like salads, tofu and fresh fruit, accompanied by a glass of Californian wine.

Safeguard yourself and your valuables. In major cities, lock your car doors while driving. At the beaches, don't carry your wallet in your back pocket.

California-speak is as casual as the lifestyle, and often includes a Mexican word or two. Say Ro-DAY-oh (Rodeo), Si-PUL-vi-dah (Sepulveda), and La Con-YAH-dah (La Cañada). But don't worry if you slip into your native tongue, you hear almost every language in the world here.

Carry a bottle of water with you at all times; "foreign" water is the "coolest."

Ceviche—a popular seafood dish

10
Good Places To Have Lunch

Gladstones 4 Fish ($$)
Fresh seafood on the beach.
✉ 17300 Pacific Coast Highway, Pacific Palisade, Los Angeles ☎ 310/GL4 FISH, 310/454 3474

The Tea Pavillion ($$)
Great views in Balboa Park accompanied by sushi, Japanese noodles and specialty teas.
✉ Balboa Pk, San Diego
☎ 619/231 0048

Pinks Hot Dog Stand ($)
Grunge stand with limo parking and great dogs and burgers.
✉ Highland and Melrose, Los Angeles

Clementine ($)
Breakfast/lunch café near Century City.
✉ 1751 Ensley Avenue, Los Angeles ☎ 310/552 1080

Karl Strauss' Old Columbia Brewery & Grill ($$)
Specialties are burgers, fresh fish and German-style sausage. Watch the microbrewery process while you sip a cold one.

✉ 1157 Columbia Street, San Diego ☎ 619/234 2739

Dottie's True Blue Café ($)
Lunch/breakfast choices.
✉ 552 Jones Street, San Francisco ☎ 415/885 2767

Gabriella Café ($$)
Californian/Italian cuisine.
✉ 910 Cedar Street, Santa Cruz ☎ 831/457 1677

Pier 23 Café ($$)
✉ The Embarcadero (Pier 23) at Broadway, San Francisco ☎ 415/362 5125

Tarpy's Roadhouse ($$)
Steak, seafood and American comfort food.
✉ 2999 Monterey-Salinas Highway, Monterey ☎ 831/647 1444

Fat City Café and Bar ($–$$)
Art nouveau, old European atmosphere with stained glass and a 100-year-old bar. Light entrées and rich desserts. ✉ 1001 Front Street, Sacramento ☎ 916/446 6769

Top Activities

- **Surfing**
- **Exercising** at a gym or health club, or by doing yoga, pilates or ta'i chi
- **Hiking/backpacking**
- **Going to the movies**
- **Cycling**
- **Rollerblading**
- **Boating** (all kinds)
- **Golfing**
- **Going to the** theme parks
- **Attending concerts** from rock to jazz to classical

10
Unique Annual Events

- National Date Festival and Fair (camel and ostrich races), Indio, February (☎ 760/863 8247)
- Snowfest (West's largest), Tahoe City, March (☎ 530/546 5253)
- Mendocino/Fort Bragg Whale Festival, March (☎ 707/961 6300)
- Frog Jumping Contest, Angel's Camp, May (☎ 209/736 2561)
- Dixieland Jazz Jubilee, Sacramento, May (☎ 916/372 5277)
- Great Monterey Squid Festival, Monterey, May (☎ 831/649 6544)
- Gilroy Garlic Festival, Gilroy, July (☎ 408/842 1625)
- Grand National Rodeo, Horse, and Stock Show, Daly City (world-class),

October (☎ 415/404 4100)
- Doo Dah Parade (spoof of famous Rose Parade), Pasadena, November (☎ 626/440 7379)
- Monarch butterfly migration to Pismo Beach's Butterfly Trees, November to March

10
California Specialties

- Sit-ins
- Sun and surf
- San Francisco hippies
- Spiritual seekers
- Sonoma and Napa Valley wines
- Stars (human, not celestial)
- Smog
- Smoking prohibitions
- San Andreas fault
- Sequoias

Rafting on the Stanislaus River

✚ 69D2
Carnegie Art Museum
✉ 424 S "C" Street
☎ 805/385 8157
🕐 Thu–Sat 10–5, Sun 1–5
✋ Inexpensive

Ventura County Gull Wings Children's Museum
✉ 418 W 4th Street
☎ 805/483 3005
🕐 Tue–Sat 10–5
✋ Inexpensive

✚ 69E1

Anza-Borrego Desert State Park
✉ Visitors Center, 2 miles (3.2km) west of Borrego Springs Township
☎ 760/767 5311
🕐 Call for hours and more information
✋ Inexpensive

Agua Caliente Indian Reservation
☎ 760/323 0151
🕐 Wed–Sat 10–5, Sun noon–5 (shorter hours in summer)
✋ Inexpensive

Palm Springs Aerial Tramway
✉ Tramway Road, 3 miles (5km) southwest of SR 111
☎ 760/325 1391
🕐 Mon–Fri 10–8, Sat–Sun 8–8. Closed 2 weeks in Aug
✋ Expensive

Resident of the Agua Caliente Indian Reservation

OXNARD ✪

Oxnard is a harbor town located on the Ventura–Los Angeles county line, and is home to an annual Strawberry Festival each May. Surpisingly overlooked by visitors are the 7 miles (11km) of beautiful beaches lining the town.

The **Carnegie Art Museum** has a permanent collection of 20th-century California painters, while changing exhibits feature photography and sculpture, with some shows spotlighting local artists.

The **Ventura County Gull Wings Children's Museum**'s hands-on exhibits of fossils and minerals, including a puppet theater and make-believe campground, will entertain the kids.

PALM SPRINGS ✪✪✪

Rising out of the desert like on oasis, Palm Springs is one of the most famous resort towns in the world. It has become a favorite of wealthy retirees with a penchant for good golf and bad driving habits, and an ever-increasing number of young people are looking here for a brief spring retreat from their studies. The summers are insufferably hot, however, and the population dwindles from June through early September.

Anza-Borrego Desert State Park offers spectacular desert scenery. Set in 600,000 acres (242,915ha), the park's main flora includes lupine, poppy, dune primrose, desert sunflower and desert lily. A variety of short trails and camp-grounds can be found here.

Five miles (8km) south of Palm Springs is **Agua Caliente Indian Reservation**. The Tribal Council here has opened part of the reservation for hiking and picnics.

An awesome view of the San Jacinto Mountains awaits if you ride the **Palm Springs Aerial Tramway**, almost 5,000ft (1,524m) straight up. The perfect way to escape the debilitating summer heat, you ride up to the wooded trails and campgrounds at the top, where refreshments are available.

PETALUMA ⭐⭐

Petaluma is another one of the quintessential small California towns. Situated on the Petaluma River, it has retained most of its 19th-century architecture and, like Modesto (➤ 76), has become a favorite for filming television series and movies.

Philanthropist Andrew Carnegie endowed $12,500 toward the construction of the **Historical Museum/ Library** in 1903. It houses permanent and rotating exhibits of early 19th-century Petaluma.

REDWOOD NATIONAL PARK (➤ 25, TOP TEN)

RIVERSIDE ⭐

Because the region has the ideal climate and soil for growing navel oranges, this was the wealthiest US city per capita and the metropolitan center of Southern California at the turn of the century. Several buildings remain from around this time: the Italian Renaissance-style City Hall, the Classic Revival municipal museum, and many exquisite Victorian homes. In addition, mission architecture and adobe residences still reflect the early wealth and prestige.

California Citrus State Historic Park features a grove of 80 varieties of citrus trees. The visitor center is a Victorian house typical of the city's heyday era. The Riverside Municipal Museum, at 3720 Orange Street, traces the history of citrus-growing in the region.

➕ 68B4

Petaluma Historical Museum/Library
✉ 20 4th Street
☎ 707/778 4398
🕐 Wed–Sat 10–4, Sun noon–3
💵 Inexpensive

➕ 69D1

California Citrus State Historic Park
✉ Van Buren Boulevard at Dufferin Avenue
☎ 951/780 6222
🕐 Daily 8–5 (until 7 Apr–Sep); visitor center Wed, Sat, Sun 10–4
🍴 Picnic facilities
💵 Free

Palm Springs Aerial Tramway

The carefully restored State Capitol Building, centre of California's government

68C4

Governor's Mansion State Historic Park
- 16th and "H" streets
- 916/323 3047
- Daily 10–4
- Inexpensive

Spirit of Sacramento
- Old Sacramento's "L" Street Landing
- 916/552 2933
- Cruises: lunch, brunch, happy hour, dinner, sunset and sightseeing
- Dinner, brunch and happy hour cruises available
- Moderate

Discovery Museum
- 101 "I" Street
- 916/264 7057
- Summer daily 10–5; winter Tue–Sun 10–5
- Inexpensive

California State Railroad Museum
- Second and "I" streets
- 916/445 6645
- Daily 10–5
- Moderate

State Capitol
- Between 10th, 15h, "L" and "N" streets
- 916/324 0333
- Tours daily 9–4
- Free

Sutter's Fort
- 27th and "L" streets
- 916/445 4422
- Daily 10–5
- Inexpensive

Sacramento Zoo
- 3930 Westland Park Drive
- 916/2264 5885
- Daily 9–4 (10–4 Nov–end Jan)
- Moderate

SACRAMENTO ✪✪

Sacramento was once a major supply center for the California '49ers (gold seekers); now it is the state capital. The names of 5,822 Californians killed in the Vietnam War are engraved on the 22 black granite panels of the California Vietnam Veterans Memorial, near the State Capitol Park.

The exquisite **Governor's Mansion** dates from the 1800s and is now a museum of Victoriana. Items from former governors include a 1902 Steinway piano and Persian carpets.

The Historic Paddlewheeler *Spirit of Sacramento* is available for a Sacramento River cruise or special events. The boat's murder-mystery trips on the *Spirit* are especially popular.

A million-dollar gold collection, ethnic photos and a historic print shop are just some of the items in the five separate areas of the **Discovery Museum**. The **California State Railroad Museum** has three entire floors devoted to railroad-related exhibits, including train cars and 21 locomotives.

Noted for its 210-ft (64-m) dome, the **State Capitol** building is nearly 150 years old, and is open daily for tours. Adobe-style **Sutter's Fort** was the first European outpost in California and contains some interesting period relics.

Sacramento Zoo has a large reptile display and 350 species of wild animals.

The Towe Ford Museum and Waterworld USA (► 111) are also worth visiting.

SALINAS

John Steinbeck was born in this working-class town 17 miles (27km) inland from Monterey, now home to the National Steinbeck Center. While it's sometimes overlooked in favor of its more affluent neighbors, Salinas is charming. For those visiting in August, there is the Steinbeck Festival. Many rodeo fans visit the town in July to catch one of the major stops on the professional rodeo circuit.

The *Hat In Three Stages of Landing* is a unique giant sculpture by Claes Oldenberg which captures a trio of bright yellow hats, each weighing 3,500lb (1,590kg). The sculpture graces the lawn of the Community Center where there are art exhibits and musical/theatrical performances.

SAN JOSE

San Jose is the 11th largest city in the US. It was founded in the last quarter of the 18th century as El Pueblo de San Jose, and is the oldest Spanish civilian settlement. From 1849 to 1851 it served as the state's capital.

Kelley Park, apart from being a popular city park with such attractions as Happy Hollow family play area and zoo, also contains the Japanese Friendship Garden and Teahouse and the San Jose Historical Museum.

Babylonian, Sumerian and Assyrian artifacts, mummies, sculptures and more can be found at the **Rosicrucian Egyptian Museum and Planetarium**. There is also a contemporary art gallery.

The **Winchester Mystery House**, a Victorian mansion and home of eccentric firearms heiress, Sarah Winchester, was designed to confuse evil spirits. The layout of the house is so complex, with blind closets, secret passageways, 13 bathrooms and 40 staircases, that even Sarah herself needed a map to find her way around. Over looking the Santa Clara Valley from the 4,209-ft (1,283-m) summit of Mount Hamilton is the **Lick Observatory**.

✚ 68B3

National Steinbeck Center
✉ 1 Main Street
☎ 831/796 3833;
www.steinbeck.org
🕐 Daily 10–5, closed major holidays
💰 Moderate

✚ 68B3

Kelley Park
✉ Senter and Story roads
🕐 Daily 8 to 30 minutes before dusk
🍴 Picnic facilities
💰 Inexpensive

Rosicrucian Egyptian Museum and Planetarium
✉ 1342 Naglee Avenue
☎ 408/947 3636
🕐 Mon–Fri 10–5, Sat–Sun 11–6
💰 Moderate; senior/student rates

Winchester Mystery House
✉ 525 S Winchester Boulevard
☎ 408/247 2101
🕐 Daily from 9am, closing times vary with time of year
💰 Expensive

Lick Observatory
✉ Mount Hamilton Road
☎ 408/274 5061
🕐 Mon–Fri 12.30–5, Sat–Sun 10–5
🍴 No nearby food or auto services
💰 Free

The bizarre Winchester House—a maze but well worth the tour price

85

✚ 69E1

Bowers Museum of Cultural Art
✉ 2002 N Main Street
☎ 714/567 3600
◷ Tue–Sun 11–4
💰 Inexpensive

SANTA ANA

A typical thriving small city in Orange County, Santa Ana centers around the South Coast Plaza, a European-styled mall with shops, restaurants and cinemas. The **Bowers Museum of Cultural Art**, a mission-style museum, is the largest in Orange County. It focuses on American, Pacific and African art, with an impressive permanent collection and quarterly visiting exhibits.

Mission Santa Barbara, often called the Queen of the Missions

✚ 68C2
El Presidio de Santa Barbara State Historic Park
✉ 122–129 E Canon Perdido Street
☎ 805/965 0093
◷ Phone for opening hours
💰 Free

Mission Santa Barbara
✉ E Los Olivos and Laguna Street
☎ 805/682 4149
◷ Daily 9–5; closed major holidays
💰 Inexpensive, under 16 free

Museum of Art
✉ 1130 State Street
☎ 805/963 4364
◷ Tue–Sun 11–5
💰 Moderate. Free Sun

SANTA BARBARA

A pleasant and affordable day trip from Los Angeles by train (moderate cost) taking you along the Pacific coast in the morning, gives you time to explore the historic adobes and museums. Lunch on Stearns Wharf, explore the specialty shops there, then stroll the white-sand beach, or play a short round of golf before returning in late afternoon. The County Courthouse, on Anacapa Street, is one of the best examples of Spanish-Moorish architecture in the US.

El Presidio de Santa Barbara State Historic Park, on the site of a late-1700 Spanish outpost, includes historical buildings such as El Cuartel, the second-oldest surviving edifice in California.

Mission Santa Barbara is the best preserved of the 21 California missions, and the church is filled with Mexican art from the 18th and 19th centuries. A Moorish fountain from 1808 graces the front and the mission is the site of The Little Fiesta each August.

The **Santa Barbara Museum of Art** has a wide variety of American, Asian and 19th-century French, Greek and Roman antiquities, including a major photographic collection.

Visit the Zoological Gardens which are natural habitats for 600 animals, and feature over 80 exhibits.

SIMI VALLEY ★★
The main reason for visiting Simi Valley is to see the **Ronald Reagan Presidential Library**, set in a beautiful, Spanish mission-style, hilltop mansion. Among the exhibits are photographs and memorabilia of the former US president's life, a full-scale replica of the Oval Office and a large portion of the Berlin Wall.

SOLEDAD ★
Soledad, the oldest settlement in the Salinas Valley, was established in 1791 with the founding of **Mission Nuestra Señora de la Soledad**, 3 miles (5km) west on US 101. The ruins of this adobe mission, along with a restored chapel and museum, can be seen to the east of town.

SOLVANG ★★★
Denmark in California might best describe Solvang, with its Danish architecture, windmills, gaslights and cobblestone walks. A tour of Solvang is possible in a horse-drawn Danish streetcar, and the town hosts several remarkable festivals annually. Contrasting the Scandinavian motif is the **Old Mission Santa Ines**, founded in 1804.

VENTURA ★
This small beach town between Los Angeles and Santa Barbara is worth a brief visit.

San Buenaventura Mission was founded in 1782. The church is restored and the museum exhibits Native American artifacts from the Chumash tribes.

Albinger Archaeological Museum displays over 3,500 years of remains, all from areas around the Mission, while Ventura County Museum of History and Art has Native American, Hispanic and pioneer exhibits.

 69D2
Ronald Reagan Presidential Library
- ✉ 40 Presidential Drive
- ☎ 800/410 8354
- 🕐 Daily 10–5; closed major holidays
- 🎟 Inexpensive

 68C3
Mission Nuestra Senora de la Soledad
- ✉ Fort Romie Road
- ☎ 831/678 2586
- 🕐 Daily 10–4
- 🎟 Donations

🏠 68C2
- ✉ Chamber of Commerce, 1693 Mission Drive
- ☎ 805/688 0701 or 800/468 6765
- 🍴 Scandinavian restaurants and cafés ($–$$$)

Old Mission Santa Ines
- ✉ 1760 Mission Drive
- ☎ 805/688 4815
- 🕐 Summer 9–6, Oct–end May 9–5.30; closed major holidays
- 🎟 Inexpensive

Typical Solvang architecture

🏠 69D2

San Buenaventura Mission
- ✉ 211 East Main Street
- ☎ 805/643 4318
- 🕐 Mon–Fri 10–5, Sat 9–5, Sun 10–4; closed major holidays
- 🎟 Inexpensive

➕ 68B4

Napa Valley Visitors Bureau

✉ 1310 Napa Town Center, Napa 94559

☎ 707/226 7459

🕐 Hours vary; some tours require reservations

Sonoma Valley Visitors Bureau

✉ 453 1st Street, E Sonoma

☎ 707/996 1090

🕐 Daily 9–5

Napa Valley Wine Train

☎ 707/253 2111 or 800/427 4124

🕐 Year-round

🎫 Expensive, reservations and deposit required

THE WINE COUNTRY

North of San Francisco lie some of the most lush valleys in all of California, the best known of which are the Napa (► 24) and Sonoma Valleys. It is here that California's vintners tend their grape vines and produce the many varied wines known and enjoyed world-wide. Whether you are driving, bicycling, taking the Wine Train or flying over the area in one of the many hot air balloons that offer spectacular views of the verdant, rolling, wine lands, you will never forget your excursion to the Wine Country.

The estates of the wineries are incredible to see. Take one of the guided tours of the processing facilities with their informative, enticing tastings. While the large wineries are the most popular, don't pass up the small, family-owned ones, of which there are many. Most have wines that rival the greats, with more convivial atmospheres.

The Napa Valley Wine Train provides daily excursions through the Napa Valley. The 1917 Pullman Dining Car relives the gracious era of elegant rail travel and distinguished service and makes you feel as if you're riding the Orient Express as the three-hour, 36-mile (58-km) trip between Napa and St. Helena allows for a leisurely brunch, lunch or dinner. Many concerns are aired by residents that the wineries are a bit too commercial for the area, but there are rarely complaints from the visitors.

To the west, the Sonoma Valley runs for 15 miles (24km) and is a bit less populated than the Napa Valley. As a rule, the 30 or so wineries here offer more personalized tours, with free tastings and a more relaxed atmosphere. The town of Sonoma itself is a good place to start if you wish to visit the valley. The other center of activity is Santa Rosa, to the north of the region.

The Sonoma Valley is particularly rich in Spanish and Mexican history, so be sure to take note of the area's beautiful architecture.

If you're looking for souvenirs of your visit to California, the on-site gift shops have unique offerings and superb wines they will ship anywhere in the world. The wineries listed are just some of the ones you'll want to explore. *Spotlight's Wine Guide* is a complete guide to the area (☎ 415/898 7908).

Above: *Reaping the rewards of a perfect climate.* Opposite: *Harvesting grapes in Alexander Valley, Sonoma*

BERINGER VINEYARDS

Beringer was one of the very first wineries to open its cellar doors to visitors. The staff here are especially attentive and knowledgeable in discussing the process of wine making and its history. There are regular tours throughout the day.

✉ Just north of downtown St. Helena, 2000 Main Street
☎ 707/963 7115
⏰ Hours and tours vary, phone for information

BUENA VISTA WINERY

As the site of the first vineyard in the valley, Buena Vista, 2 miles (3km) northeast of Sonoma, has become a historical landmark. The wine cellars, built in 1857, are the oldest stone cellars in the state. The Tasting Room offers selection of award-winning wines and there is a gift shop, a picnic area, an artists' gallery, self-guided tours and historical presentations.

✉ 18000 Old Winery Road
☎ 707/938 1266
⏰ Daily 10–5

KENWOOD VINEYARDS

Operating on Jack London's former ranch since 1970, this Sonoma country winery produces Cabernet Sauvignon, Zinfandel, Sauvignon Blanc, Chardonnay, Gewürztraminer, Merlot and Pinot Noir on the estate which is about 1-hour's drive north of San Francisco. Visitors can sample up to four wines, which are produced from grapes grown on site and sourced from local vineyards, and can hike and take bicycle rides around the property.

✉ 9592 Sonoma Highway (Highway 12), Kenwood
☎ 707/833 5891
⏰ Daily 10–4.30

Did you know ?

Over a century ago, Hungarian Agoston Haraszthy planted the first vineyard in California, near the small town of Sonoma, seeding it with the best European grapes he could find. The state gave him funding, but neither envisioned the huge industry that would spring from his venture.

A Walk in Sequoia National Park

Distance
5 miles (8km)

Time
2–4 hours

Start point
General Sherman Tree
✚ 69D3

End point
General Sherman or Long Meadow
✚ 69D3

Lunch
Grant Grove Restaurant ($$)
✉ Grant Grove Visitors Center
☎ 559/335 5500, ext 306

Whole groves of giants flourish in Sequoia

This walk takes you through the forest of Sequoia National Park. Even if you visit during the heat of the summer, you will find the temperatures comfortably cool because of the towering foliage.

Begin at the General Sherman Tree, 2 miles (3.2km) east of Giant Forest Village.

The General Sherman tree (named for the Civil War general) is 275ft (84m) high. It is estimated to be more than 2,500 years old and contains enough wood to build 40 houses.

Walk down the self-guided, paved Congress Trail. Cross Sherman Creek on the quaint wooden bridge.

Experience the awesome giant sequoias, like the character-laden Leaning Tree and some lightning-struck and fire-scarred trees as well.

About a mile (1.6km) further, you will meet the junction with the Alta Trail and a grove known as The Senate. A little further along the fern-filled trail is The House Grove.

These two stands are named after the two governing bodies of the United States government. The path also visits the McKinley Tree (named for the US president). After World War II, the practice of naming big trees after politicos was abandoned.

Continue a half-mile (0.8km) back, and return to the trail head. For a longer hike (about 6 miles/10km), follow the Congress Trail to the junction of The Trail of the Sequoias. Take this path for a half-mile (0.8km) to the hike's high point, then gradually descend one and a half miles (2.5km) into Long Meadow.

Lunch before, or after, your hike at Giant Forest Village.

Where To...

Above: *City Lights
bookstore, North
Beach*
Right: *Fisherman's
Wharf is the place to
go for fresh seafood
in San Francisco*

San Francisco

Prices

Average meal per head excluding drink:

$ = up to $15
$$ = between $15 and $30
$$$ = over $30

Good Old Dishes

The local cuisine of San Francisco dates back to the Gold Rush days. Old faithful dishes such as cioppino (seafood casserole), hangtown fry (oysters dipped in egg and flour and fried with bacon), fortune cookies and Irish coffee are among the most famous. Most fresh fish is grilled with a bit of Slavic, or French, influence.

Diamond Ratings

AAA tourism editors evaluate and rate each restaurant on the overall quality of food, sevice, decor and ambience—with extra emphasis given to food and service. Ratings range from one diamond indicating a simple family-oriented establishment to five diamonds indicating an establishment offering superb culinary skills and an ultimate dining experience.

Alfred's ($$)

Quintessential steakhouse with bordello-like setting. Portions to suit big appetites.

✉ **659 Merchant Street, between Kearny and Montgomery streets** ☎ **415/781 7058** 🕐 **Lunch, dinner**

Aqua ($$$)

Glamorous downtown restaurant serving French-American gourmet seafood.

✉ **252 California Street** ☎ **415/956 9662** 🕐 **Lunch, dinner**

Balboa Cafe ($$)

Trendy café with a traditional American menu. The place to "see and be seen."

✉ **3199 Fillmore Street** ☎ **415/921 3944** 🕐 **Lunch, dinner**

Betelnut ($$)

Lively atmosphere, tropical drinks and pan-Asian fare, with elements of Thai, Chinese and Korean cuisine.

✉ **2030 Union Street** ☎ **415/929 8855** 🕐 **Lunch, dinner**

Bix ($$$)

Martinis, cigar smoke, upscale crowd and great steaks and seafood make this one of San Francisco's most popular restaurants. Reservations recommended.

✉ **56 Gold Street, between Montgomery and Sansome streets** ☎ **415/433 6300** 🕐 **Dinner; lunch Fri only**

Caffe Sport ($$)

Italian restaurant, a favorite with North Beach regulars. Sicilian specialties.

✉ **574 Green Street** ☎ **415/981 1251** 🕐 **Lunch, dinner; closed Sun, Mon; no credit cards**

Le Charm ($$)

French bistro and garden with terrific prix fixe menu.

✉ **315 5th Street** ☎ **415/546 6128** 🕐 **Lunch, dinner**

Dottie's True Blue Cafe ($)

Great diner for typical American food. Home-style atmosphere and affordable prices make it a hit.

✉ **522 Jones Street** ☎ **415/885 2767** 🕐 **Breakfast, lunch; closed Tue**

Ebisu ($$)

Top-rated sushi and traditional Asian food. You may have to wait but its worth it.

✉ **1283 Ninth Avenue** ☎ **415/566 1770** 🕐 **Lunch, dinner**

Firefly ($$)

Local favorite for home cooking and friendly service. Great place to people watch.

✉ **4288 24th Street** ☎ **415/821 7652** 🕐 **Lunch, dinner**

Fleur de Lys ($$$)

The city's most romantic restaurant. Attentive service and superb contemporary French food.

✉ **777 Sutter Street** ☎ **415/673 7779** 🕐 **Lunch, dinner; closed Sun**

Fog City Diner ($$)

Upscale '50s-style diner on Telegraph Hill. American and seafood specialties.

✉ **1300 Battery Street** ☎ **415/982 2000** 🕐 **Lunch, dinner**

Gary Danko ($$$)

Romantic Russian Hill/wharf restaurant featuring French-Californian fare. Diners can design their own three- to five-course meal. Pricey, but worth it.

✉ **800 N Point Street**
☎ 415/749 2060 🕐 Dinner only

The House ($$)
Quaint and quiet with superb food Asian-American cuisine at a moderate price.
✉ **1230 Grant Avenue** ☎ 415/986 8612 🕐 Lunch, dinner

🍷🍷🍷Jeanty at Jacks ($$)
Opened in 1864, this historic restaurant has a new owner and a new French menu.
✉ **615 Sacramento Street** ☎ 415/693 0941 🕐 Lunch, dinner

Kate's Kitchen ($)
Authentic, inexpensive "soul" food in the famous Haight-Ashbury district. Great for breakfast or late-night dining.
✉ **471 Haight Street** ☎ 415/626 3984 🕐 Breakfast, lunch, dinner; no credit cards

🍷🍷Lulu ($$)
Innovative, Mediterranean bistro located in a large converted warehouse. Family-style service with excellent food.
✉ **816 Folsom** ☎ 415/495 5775 🕐 Lunch, dinner

The Mandarin ($$$)
Long-time favorite for great views and exotic environment. Chinese cuisine; specializes in Peking duck.
✉ **900 N Point Street** ☎ 415/673 8812 🕐 Lunch, dinner

Mel's Drive In ($)
A revival of the popular 1950s-style drive-in. Top-rated burgers, fries and milk shakes and, of course, a great jukebox.
✉ **2165 Lombard Street** ☎ 415/921 2867; ✉ **3355**

Geary Street ☎ 415/387 2244;
✉ **801 Mission Street** ☎ 415/227 4477 🕐 Lunch, dinner, open late

🍷🍷L'Osteria del Forno ($$)
Northern Italian cuisine in North Beach. Expect a long wait, as the restaurant is tiny and the food delicious.
✉ **519 Columbus Avenue** ☎ 415/982 1124 🕐 Lunch, dinner; closed Tue; no credit cards

Perry's ($)
Local watering hole, so popular with the young set that they added a second location. Good American food and a comfortable ambience.
✉ **1944 Union Street** ☎ 415/922 9022; ✉ **185 Sutter Street** ☎ 415/989 6895 🕐 Lunch, dinner

🍷🍷🍷PlumpJack Cafe ($$)
"Hot spot" specializing in American food. Offers top-notch wine list. Reservations may be difficult to get, but you'll be glad you persisted.
✉ **3127 Fillmore Street** ☎ 415/563 4755 🕐 Lunch, dinner

🍷🍷🍷Slanted Door ($$$)
Creative Vietnamese food accompanied by a fantastic view of the Bay Bridge.
✉ **Ferry Building, 1 Ferry Plaza** ☎ 415/861 8032 🕐 Lunch, dinner

Swan Oyster Depot ($$)
Unique seafood emporium in operation since 1912. Service from an old-fashioned marble bar.
✉ **1517 Polk Street** ☎ 415/673 1101 🕐 Lunch, dinner; closed Sun; no credit cards

Diversity
The strength of any great city is the diversity of its cuisine and restaurants. San Francisco certainly flexes its muscles in this respect. The most elegant restaurants are located in the center of the city. By region, the best Italian can be found in the North Beach area, while Latin dishes are the highlights in the Mission District. Chinatown offers Asian restaurants, naturally, from Thai to Vietnamese to Cambodian.

Los Angeles

Ethnic Mix

Los Angeles restaurants reflect the city's diverse ethnic mix. Tail-o-the-Pup hot dog stand (San Vicente & Beverly) combines architectural uniqueness with a great dog, and just a couple of blocks away, La Cienega Boulevard's "restaurant row" offers eateries for every taste and budget. Because smoking is prohibited in Los Angeles County restaurants and the weather is gorgeous year-round, patio dining is nouvelle vogue.

Apple Pan ($)

A throwback to the 1940s (authentic) this LA institution serves fresh, juicy hamburgers, tasty fries and pie at a burger counter.
✉ 10801 W Pico Boulevard ☎ 310/475 3585 ⏰ Lunch, dinner; closed Mon

Border Grill ($$)

Hip cantina by the beach. Serves exotic Mexican specialties. Stylish ambience; great margaritas.
✉ 1445 4th Street, Santa Monica ☎ 310/451 1655 ⏰ Lunch, dinner

Buffalo Club ($$$)

Westside club/restaurant, with top-notch American cuisine.
✉ 1520 Olympic Boulevard (at 15th Street) ☎ 310/450 8600 ⏰ Lunch, dinner

🍷🍷Café Talesai ($$)

Fresh and natural ingredients at this hip Thai place, located in a mall. Try the hidden treasures signature appetizer.
✉ 9198 Olympic Boulevard ☎ 310/271 9345 ⏰ Lunch Mon–Fri, dinner daily

Cheesecake Factory ($)

One of the most popular restaurants in Southern California because of its huge portions of traditional American fare and a gauntlet of cheesecake.
✉ 364 N Beverly Drive, Beverly Hills ☎ 310/278 7270 ✉ 4142 Via Marina, Marina del Rey ☎ 310/306 3344 ⏰ Lunch, dinner

Dan Tana's ($$$)

Long-time celebrity hangout for Italian food, the best steaks and fresh lobster. *Very* Hollywood.
✉ 9071 Santa Monica Boulevard ☎ 310/275 9444 ⏰ Dinner only, but open late

Duke's ($)

Sunset Strip coffee shop/diner where fantastic omelettes attract the young and hip. Long lines at breakfast, especially on weekends.
✉ 8909 Sunset Boulevard ☎ 310/652 3100 ⏰ Breakfast, lunch, dinner

🍷🍷El Cholo ($$)

Long-established family-owned Mexican serving traditional fare since 1927. Another location is in Santa Monica.
✉ 1121 S Western Avenue ☎ 323/734 2773 ⏰ Lunch, dinner

🍷🍷🍷The Ivy ($$$)

Great American food and the place to see and be seen in LA. Outdoor patio. To ensure a table reservations are a must.
✉ 113 N Robertson Boulevard ☎ 310/274 8303 ⏰ Lunch, dinner

🍷🍷🍷Lawry's Prime Rib ($$$)

The best for prime rib anywhere, supposedly, in the world. "To die for," says one. You decide, but make reservations early.
✉ 100 N La Cienega ☎ 866/223 8224 ⏰ Dinner only

🍷🍷🍷Maple Drive ($$$)

Well-known Beverly Hills celebrity-owned restaurant. American menu and pleasing jazz.
✉ 345 N Maple Drive, Beverly Hills ☎ 310/274 9800 ⏰ Lunch, dinner; closed Sun

Matsuhisa ($$$)
The flagship restaurant of the growing Nobu empire, Matsuhisa serves fantastic sushi and sashimi in a bustling, intimate setting.
✉ 129 N La Cienega ☎ 310/659 9639 🕐 Lunch Mon–Fri, dinner daily

Musso and Frank ($$)
A touch of "Old Hollywood" serving traditional fare. Great martinis and the best Caesar salad in LA.
✉ 6667 Hollywood Boulevard ☎ 323/467 7788 🕐 Lunch, dinner; closed Sun, Mon

L'Orangerie ($$$)
Modern-classic French food. Impeccable service; terrace dining. Consistently in California's top listings. Dress code.
✉ 903 N La Cienega Boulevard ☎ 310/652 9770 🕐 Dinner only; closed Sun, Mon

Pacific Dining Car ($$$)
Downtown standard for steaks and seafood. Draws day-time business crowd but is best in the evening. Reservations recommended.
✉ 1310 W 6th Street ☎ 213/483 6000 🕐 Breakfast, lunch, dinner

Parkway Grill ($$)
The continental cuisine is worth the trip to Pasadena. Also California fare.
✉ 510 S Arroyo Parkway, Pasadena ☎ 626/795 1001 🕐 Lunch Mon–Fri, dinner daily

Patina ($$$)
Comfortable and unpretentious French bistro.
✉ 141 S Grand Avenue ☎ 213/972 3331 🕐 Lunch, dinner

Roscoe's House of Chicken and Waffles ($)
Famous with locals for its informal setting, sinfully greasy chicken and delectable waffles any time of day. Several locations.
✉ 1514 N Gower Street (at Sunset Boulevard) ☎ 323/466 7453 🕐 Breakfast, lunch, dinner, open late

Spago ($$$)
World-renowned for chef Wolfgang Puck's gourmet pizzas, and its star-studded Academy Awards party. Also fine California cuisine.
✉ 176 N Canon Drive ☎ 310/385 0880 🕐 Dinner only

Surya India ($$)
Samosas, tandoori and curries near the farmers' market.
✉ 8048 W 3rd Street ☎ 323/653 5151 🕐 Lunch, dinner

Tommy's Original Hamburger ($)
Perhaps the greatest hamburger stand on the planet. Greasy, but great!
✉ 2575 Beverly Boulevard ☎ 213/389 9060 🕐 Daily 24hrs; no credit cards

Trattoria Farfalla ($)
Italian café serving great thin-crust pizzas. Usually crowded, but worth the wait.
✉ 1978 N Hillhurst Street, Los Feliz ☎ 323/661 7365 🕐 Lunch, dinner

Valentino ($$$)
Elegant, expensive Italian, with a great wine list and impeccable service. Reservations required.
✉ 3115 Pico Boulevard, Santa Monica ☎ 310/829 4313 🕐 Dinner; lunch only on Fri; closed Sun

People-watching
California was at the forefront of the coffee-house and health food restaurants craze. It is also the state where "hanging out" and "people-watching" have been elevated to an art form. Sunset Plaza (West Hollywood), Ventura Boulevard (San Fernando Valley), La Brea (Hollywood), Melrose Avenue (Hollywood), and the beaches in Venice, Santa Monica and Malibu are exceptional areas to go when you wish to sit, feed and watch.

San Diego

Whatever You Choose
San Diego's restaurants are known for their emphasis on seafood and South-of-the-Border cuisine. The Downtown, Old Town and Hillcrest sections offer the most diverse choices of dining and ambience. Other areas that offer cafés, coffeehouses, diners and fine dining are Ocean Beach, Point Loma, Coronado, Mission Beach and Pacific Beach. The San Diego area also has a great many health food and vegetarian restaurants.

🍷🍷🍷Anthony's Star of the Sea Room ($$$)
Family-owned seafood restaurant. Great service, beautiful harbor views. Jacket required.
✉ 1360 Harbor Drive ☎ 619/232 5103 🕐 Lunch, dinner

Athens Market ($$)
No-frills Greek restaurant. Belly dancers on weekends.
✉ 109 W F Street ☎ 619/234 1955 🕐 Lunch Mon–Fri, dinner daily

Cafe Lulu ($)
Coffeehouse/restaurant in the Gaslamp Quarter neighborhood. One of the few late-night places to eat.
✉ 419 F Street ☎ 619/238 0114 🕐 Breakfast, lunch, dinner; no credit cards

🍷🍷🍷Café Pacifica ($$)
Good seafood specialties in unique, old cemetery setting.
✉ 2414 San Diego Avenue, Old Town ☎ 619/291 6666 🕐 Dinner only

🍷City Delicatessen ($)
Centrally located Jewish deli.
✉ 535 University Avenue ☎ 619/295 2747 🕐 Breakfast, lunch, dinner, open late

Dakota ($)
Mesquite-grilled fish and fowl at good prices. Live music.
✉ 901 5th Avenue ☎ 619/234 5554 🕐 Lunch Mon–Fri, dinner daily

Dick's Last Resort ($)
Continental dining in a converted warehouse.
✉ 345 Fourth Avenue ☎ 619/231 9100 🕐 Lunch, dinner

Le Fontainebleau ($$$)
Expensive French restaurant in The Westgate Hotel. Offers gallery of original oil paintings and award-winning seafood and veal. Pianist.
✉ 1055 Second Avenue ☎ 619/557 3655 🕐 Lunch, dinner

🍷🍷Hob Nob Hill ($$)
Family-owned and open since World War II. Specialties include fried scallops and rack of lamb. Kids' menu.
✉ 2271 First Avenue (near Balboa Park) ☎ 619/239 8176 🕐 Lunch, dinner

Kansas City Barbeque ($)
No-frills barbecue stand with lots of personality.
✉ 610 W Market Street ☎ 619/231 9680 🕐 Lunch, dinner

Old Town Mexican Cafe ($)
This café is the place for the best Mexican fare in San Diego.
✉ 2489 San Diego Avenue ☎ 619/297 4330 🕐 Breakfast, lunch, dinner

🍷🍷🍷Rainwaters on Kettner ($$$)
Private club atmosphere with standard American cuisine. Dress code enforced.
✉ 1202 Kettner Boulevard ☎ 619/233 5757 🕐 Lunch, dinner; no lunch on weekends

Thee Bungalow ($$)
This family-run French spot has seen pleasing restaurant loyalists for over 30 years.
✉ 4996 West Point Loma Boulevard ☎ 619/224 2884 🕐 Dinner daily

🍷🍷🍷Umi Sushi ($$)
Traditional sushi offerings, plus tempura, teriyaki and specials.
✉ 2806 Shelter Island Drive ☎ 619/226 1135 🕐 Lunch Mon–Sat, dinner daily

Rest of California

Eureka
♨♨Sea Grill ($$)
Extensive seafood menu that includes cod Louisiana and Hawaiian mahi-mahi.
✉ 316 "E" St, Old Town
☎ 707/443 7187 🕐 Lunch, dinner. Closed Sun

Marin County
Olema Farm House Restaurant ($$)
This shingle-sided eatery was a stagecoach stop in 1872, but today's fare is nouveau American.
✉ 10005 Highway 1, Olema
☎ 415/663 1264 🕐 Breakfast, lunch, dinner

Mendocino
♨♨Mendocino Hotel ($$$)
Cozy, antique-filled hotel. Dine in an elegant Victorian parlor or garden café. Excellent Continental cuisine and seafood specialties.
✉ 45080 Main Street ☎ 707/937 0511 🕐 Breakfast, lunch, dinner

Montecito
♨♨♨Montecito Cafe ($$)
California cuisine; warm setting in The Montecito Inn.
✉ 1295 Coast Village Road
☎ 805/969 3392 🕐 Lunch, dinner

Stonehouse ($$$)
Regional cuisine in rustic, romantic setting. At the San Ysidro Ranch Resort.
✉ 900 San Ysidro Road
☎ 805/969 5046 🕐 Lunch, dinner

Morro Bay
♨♨♨Hoppe's ($$)
International cuisine and great wine list.
✉ 78 North Ocean Avenue
☎ 805/772 9012 🕐 Lunch, dinner; closed Mon–Tue

Ojai
♨♨Suzanne's Cuisine ($$)
A real gem off the beaten path. Inexpensive California cuisine.
✉ 502 W Ojai Avenue
☎ 805/ 640 1961 🕐 Lunch, dinner; closed Tue

♨♨♨Ranch House ($$)
A lush garden patio, with meat and seafood dishes.
✉ W Lomita Avenue
☎ 805/646 2360 🕐 Dinner Tue–Sun, Sun brunch

Orange County
♨♨Antonello Risorante ($$)
A local favorite serving Northern Italian fare in an elegant setting.
✉ 3800 Plaza Drive, Santa Ana
☎ 714/751 7153 🕐 Lunch Mon–Fri, dinner Mon–Sat

♨♨♨♨Aubergine ($$$)
Classic French cuisine on the Balboa peninsula. Elegant atmosphere.
✉ 508 29th Street, Newport Beach ☎ 949/723 4150
🕐 Dinner only; closed Mon

♨♨♨Bistango ($$)
Combined restaurant and art gallery with Continental cuisine, prix fixe. Extensive wine list and nightly entertainment.
✉ 19100 Von Karman Avenue, Irvine ☎ 949/752 5222
🕐 Lunch Mon–Fri, dinner daily

Cafe Zoolu ($$)
Funky and eclectic. Known for its vegetarian delights and grilled specialties.
✉ 860 Glenneyre Street, Laguna Beach ☎ 949/494 6825
🕐 Dinner only; closed Mon

Satisfying Your Needs
Food lovers will find California like no other place on earth in its diversity and sheer number of restaurants and cafés. California has initiated such US culinary trends as sushi bars, the buzz-word nouvelle and, naturally, California cuisine. Although Mexican and South American dishes are prevalent, you can satisfy just about any food craving in the Golden State.

Ocean Views

From San Diego to the top of the state, along California Route 1, you are guaranteed to find small inns with sweeping views of the Pacific and excellent food at moderate prices. Or, for funky fun and lots of food for little money, there are also the roadhouses, like the not-to-be-missed Patrick's in Santa Monica.

Clay Oven ($)

Delightful Indian restaurant with friendly service and great prices. Good lunch buffet.

✉ **15435 Jeffrey Road (Irvine Center), Irvine** ☎ **949/552 2851** ⓒ **Lunch, dinner**

Jack Shrimp ($$)

Spicy Cajun, casual environment; moderately priced.

✉ **2400 W Coast Highway, Newport Beach** ☎ **949/650 5577** ⓒ **Lunch (Fri only), dinner**

🍷🍷Javier's ($$)

Ocean views and large portions. Try the house specialty.

✉ **480 S Coast Highway** ☎ **949/474 1239** ⓒ **Lunch, dinner**

McCharles House and Tearoom ($$)

Superb Continental menu. Famous for its desserts. Unique Victorian décor, pleasant patio under huge eucalyptus trees.

✉ **335 S "C" Street, Tustin** ☎ **714/731 4063** ⓒ **Call for opening times**

🍷🍷🍷Oysters ($$)

New and trendy place for fresh seafood and wine from the owner's vineyard. Live entertainment.

✉ **2515 E Coast Highway, Corona del Mar** ☎ **949/675 7411** ⓒ **Dinner only**

Stix ($$)

A budget Chinese restaurant offering fast but friendly service.

✉ **28251 Crown Valley Parkway, Laguna Niguel** ☎ **949/831 7849** ⓒ **Lunch, dinner**

Tangata ($$)

Continental and South-western cuisine in the Bowers Museum.

✉ **2002 N Main Street, Santa Ana** ☎ **714/550 0906** ⓒ **Lunch only Tue–Sun**

🍷🍷🍷21 Ocean Front ($$$)

A charming seafood restaurant at the foot of Newport Pier.

✉ **2100 W Oceanfront, Newport Beach** ☎ **949/673 2100** ⓒ **Dinner only**

Zinc Café and Market ($)

Stereotypical California, vegetarian coffee-house. Great muffins. Hangout of the arty set. Usually crowded, but worth the wait.

✉ **350 Ocean Avenue, Laguna Beach** ☎ **949/494 6302** ⓒ **Breakfast, lunch only**

🍷🍷🍷Zov's Bistro ($$)

Trendy, with Mediterranean cuisine and fresh bread from the on-site bakery.

✉ **17740 E 17th Street, Tustin** ☎ **714/838 8855** ⓒ **Lunch, dinner**

Palm Springs/Palm Desert

🍷La Casuelas Terraza ($)

Mexican food and fantastic margaritas in a relaxing but lively atmosphere.

✉ **222 South Palm Canyon Drive, Palm Springs** ☎ **760/325 2794** ⓒ **Lunch, dinner daily**

🍷🍷🍷Cedar Creek Inn ($$)

Home-town favorite for reliable American food.

✉ **1555 S Palm Canyon Drive** ☎ **760/325 7300**

🍷🍷🍷Cuistot ($$$

A popular and elegant restaurant featuring

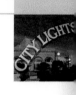

California-French cuisine. The specialties are veal and rack of lamb. Pricey but worth it.

✉ 72595 El Paseo, Palm Desert ☎ 760/340 1000 🕐 Lunch, dinner; closed Mon

▼▼▼Palm Springs Chop House ($$$)
Steaks, chops and large side orders, plus tasty desserts.

✉ 262 S Palm Canyon Drive ☎ 760/320 4500 🕐 Dinner only

▼▼▼Ristorante Mamma Gina ($$)
Authentic northern Italian with homemade pasta, chicken and veal specialties.

✉ 73–705 El Paseo Drive ☎ 760/568 9898 🕐 Lunch, dinner

San Luis Obispo
Big Sky Cafe ($)
Here you'll find Caribbean cuisine in a fun and casual environment.

✉ 1121 Broad Street ☎ 805/545 5401 🕐 Breakfast, lunch, dinner

▼▼▼Buono Tavola ($$)
A great-value Italian restaurant in a casual, country setting.

✉ 1037 Monterey Street ☎ 805/545 8000 🕐 Lunch Mon–Fri, dinner daily

Santa Barbara
Brophy Brother's Clam Bar and Restaurant ($$)
Spectacular views and an energetic crowd.

✉ 119 Harbor Way ☎ 805/966 4418 🕐 Lunch, dinner

Carlito's Cafe ($)
Budget Mexican and interesting vegetarian plates.

✉ 1324 State Street ☎ 805/962 7117 🕐 Lunch, dinner

▼▼Chucks of Hawaii ($$)
Polynesian décor and award-winning steaks and wine. Casual fun atmosphere.

✉ 3888 State Street ☎ 805/687 4417 🕐 Dinner only

▼▼▼Citronelle ($$$)
Ocean views welcome diners at this sophisticated restaurant. Interesting French and California cuisine.

✉ 901 Cabrillo Boulevard ☎ 805/963 0111 🕐 Lunch, dinner

▼▼The Hitching Post ($)
Barbecue, steaks and french fries in a casual roadhouse atmosphere.

✉ 406 E Highway 246, Buellton ☎ 805/688 0676 ✉ 3325 Point Sal Road, Casmalia ☎ 805/937 6151 🕐 Dinner only

Wine Country
Bistro Don Giovanni ($$$)
Serves Italian and Mediterranean specialties in a beautiful artistic setting. Daily pasta specials.

✉ 4110 Howard Lane, Napa ☎ 707/224 3300 🕐 Lunch, dinner

French Laundry ($$$)
Thomas Keller's famed new French restaurant. Takes reservations months in advance. Outdoor dining area. Prices are very steep.

✉ 6640 Washington Street, Yountville ☎ 707/944 2380 🕐 Lunch, dinner daily

Mustards ($$)
Napa Valley's trendiest and most popular spot for California cuisine. Reservations recommended.

✉ 7399 St Helena Highway, St. Helena ☎ 707/944 2424 🕐 Lunch, dinner

Roadside Stands
To complement California's wide range of restaurants and cuisines, an abundance of roadside stands offer fresh-picked produce and fruit. There is no better way to sample the culinary diversity of a region, and whether you want a refreshing and healthy traveling snack or an inexpensive breakfast to enjoy in your room, you'll find these roadside wares excellent value.

San Francisco

Prices

You may expect to pay the following prices per room per night.

$ = under $100
$$ = between $100 and $250
$$$ = over $250

Diamond Ratings

AAA tourism editors evaluate and rate each lodging establishment based on the overall quality and services. AAA's diamond rating criteria reflect the design and service standards set by the lodging industry. combined with the expectations of its members.

A one or two diamond rating represents a clean and well-maintained property offering comfortable rooms, with the two diamond property showing enhancements in decor and furnishings. A three diamond property shows marked upgrades in physical attributes, services and comfort and may offer additional amenities. A four diamond rating signifies a property offering a high level of service and hospitality and a wide variety of amenities and upscale facilities. A five diamond rating represents a world-class facility, offering the highest level of luxurious accommodations and personalized guest services.

◆◆◆Archbishop's Mansion ($$)

Historic 1904 bed-and-breakfast with stained-glass windows and elegant European furnishings.
✉ **1000 Fulton Street**
☎ **415/563 7872**

◆◆◆Beresford Arms Hotel ($$)

A traditional hotel with Continental breakfast. Tea, wine and snacks in the afternoon. Near Union Square.
✉ **701 Post Street** ☎ **415/673 2600** ♿ **Wheelchair access**

◆◆Comfort Inn by the Bay ($)

Near Lombard Street and the major attractions. Reasonable rates.
✉ **2775 Van Ness Avenue**
☎ **415/928 5000**
♿ **Wheelchair access**

◆◆◆The Fairmont Hotel and Tower ($$$)

Newly renovated historic hotel, situated atop Nob Hill.
✉ **950 Mason Street** ☎ **415/772 5000** ♿ **Wheelchair access**

Four Season's Clift ($$$)

This art deco hotel has Oriental carpets, chandeliers and tasteful rooms.
✉ **495 Geary Street**
☎ **415/775 4700**

◆◆◆Hotel Rex ($$$)

Near Union Square, in a style inspired by art and literary salons of the early 1900s.
✉ **562 Sutter Street**
☎ **415/433 4434**

◆◆◆Hotel Triton ($$)

Near Chinatown. Tasteful art deco design with exhibitions of local artwork in the lobby.
✉ **342 Grant Avenue**

☎ **415/ 394 0500**
♿ **Wheelchair access**

◆◆◆The Inn at the Opera ($$$)

Near Performing Arts Center. Small and elegant with first-rate service.
✉ **333 Fulton Street** ☎ **415/863 8400** ♿ **Wheelchair access**

◆◆◆ ◆◆◆Mark Hopkins Inter-Continental ($$$)

On the site of the old Mark Hopkins mansion. Offers a spectacular view of the city.
✉ **1 Nob Hill** ☎ **415/392 3434**

Mill Valley Inn ($$)

Beautiful hotel central to this small, artistic community.
✉ **165 Throckmorton Avenue, Mill Valley** ☎ **415/389 6608**

◆◆◆Queen Anne ($$)

Converted art deco style Victorian house. Complimentary breakfast, and afternoon tea and sherry; attentive staff.
✉ **1590 Sutter Street** ☎ **415/441 2828** ♿ **Wheelchair access**

◆◆◆Sir Francis Drake ($$)

Opulence with bed-and-breakfast flavor.
✉ **450 Powell Street**
☎ **415/392 7755**

◆◆◆White Swan Inn ($$–$$$)

A boutique hotel in Nob Hill, with 26 rooms and a convenient location.
✉ **845 Bush Street**
☎ **415/775 1755**

◆◆◆York Hotel ($$)

Renovated 1922 hotel. Parts of Alfred Hitchcock's *Vertigo* were filmed here.
✉ **940 Sutter Street**
☎ **415/885 6800**

Los Angeles

The Argyle ($$$)

An LA landmark; 15 stories of art deco elegance at the end of Sunset Strip. Popular movie location.

✉ 8358 Sunset Boulevard, W Hollywood ☎ 323/654 7100

Beverly Hills Hotel ($$$)

Restored in the early 1990s by its owner, the Sultan of Brunei. Known for its private bungalows and the celebrity-packed Polo Lounge.

✉ 9641 Sunset Boulevard ☎ 310/276 2251

Chateau Marmont Hotel ($$$)

Favorite of film and music communities in the style of a Loire Valley château.

✉ 8221 Sunset Boulevard ☎ 323/656 1010

Holiday Inn($$)

Reliable accommodations from this international chain.

✉ 1020 S Fiqueroa St, Downtown LA ☎ 213/748 1291

Hollywood Roosevelt ($$)

Site of first Academy Awards presentation (1927). Centrally located (► 21).

✉ 7000 Hollywood Boulevard ☎ 323/466 7000

Hotel Bel-Air ($$$)

Exotic Mediterranean-style hotel. A hideaway for the rich and famous.

✉ 701 Stone Canyon Road ☎ 310/472 1211

Hotel Sofitel ($$)

Affordable Mediterranean-style hotel. Across from the Beverly Center Mall (► 107).

✉ 8555 Beverly Boulevard ☎ 310/278 5444

Malibu Beach Inn ($$$)

Mediterranean-style hotel on a white-sand shore.

✉ 22878 Pacific Coast Highway, Malibu ☎ 310/456 6444

New Otani Hotel and Garden ($$$)

Japanese-style hotel. Beautiful gardens, well-appointed rooms.

✉ 120 S Los Angeles Street ☎ 213/629 1200

Sheraton Universal ($$$)

Views of Hollywood Hills and San Fernando Valley. Close to Universal City attractions. Good-value weekend packages.

✉ 333 Universal Hollywood Drive Parkway ☎ 818/980 1212

Shutters on the Beach ($$$)

Contemporary beachfront hotel with all the amenities. Marble bathrooms, sweeping ocean views.

✉ 1 Pico Boulevard, Santa Monica ☎ 310/458 0030

Sunset Marquis ($$$)

Mediterranean décor, mostly suites. Set on a residential street, this hotel is a favorite of the entertainment community for its casual atmosphere.

✉ 1200 N Alta Loma Road ☎ 310/657 1333

Wyndham Bel Age ($$$)

All-suite hotel in the heart of West Hollywood. Roof-top swimming pool with fantastic views of the city.

✉ 1020 N San Vicente Boulevard ☎ 310/854 1111

Convenient Location

In Los Angeles, the Westside hotels (from Hollywood to Santa Monica) are probably the best locations for those who wish to visit LA's attractions and enjoy the sights. For the best rates, inquire at the specific hotels for package deals, or call one of the many "brokers" that are emerging in the hotel industry (check local listings for names and numbers).

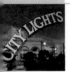

San Diego/Rest of California

Beside the Sea

The San Diego area is a great place to book into a beachside hotel or resort. The pleasing year-round climate will make it almost irresistible to spend an afternoon by the pool or at the beach. La Jolla, Del Mar and Laguna Beach are just a few areas to look into for a time of rest and relaxation in the sun. Even though winter temperatures are still nearly perfect, many hotels and inns reduce their rates.

San Diego

⚜⚜⚜Bay Club Hotel ($$$)
Large rooms, some with private balconies and patios. Situated on the Marina.
✉ 2131 Shelter Island Drive
☎ 619/224 8888

⚜⚜Comfort Inn Gaslamp ($$)
In the historic Gaslamp Quarter, and close to the zoo and Balboa Park.
✉ 660 G Street ☎ 619/238 4100

⚜⚜ ⚜⚜Coronado Marriott ($$$)
French and Californian décor on 16 acres (6ha) of exotic landscaped grounds.
✉ 2000 Second Street
☎ 619/435 3000

⚜⚜⚜Hilton San Diego ($$)
This hotel offers affordable rates near the airport.
✉ 1960 Harbor Island Drive
☎ 619/291 6700

⚜⚜⚜Horton Grand ($$$)
The oldest building in San Diego (1886). The Horton Grand has Victorian décor with an impressive lobby.
✉ 311 Island Avenue
☎ 619/544 1886

Hotel del Coronado ($$$)
Famous Victorian hotel jutting out into the bay. Large rooms, some suites. One room is "haunted."
✉ 1500 Orange Avenue
☎ 619/435 6611

⚜⚜⚜Humphrey's Half Moon Inn ($$)
Beautiful gardens and island décor overlooking the bay.
✉ 2303 Shelter Island Drive
☎ 619/224 3411

La Costa Resort and Spa ($$$)
Large, luxury resort with golf, tennis and watersports.
✉ 2100 Costa Del Mar Road, Carlsbad ☎ 760/438 9111

⚜⚜⚜⚜⚜The Lodge at Torrey Pines ($$$)
Luxurious five-star accomodations in La Jolla. Overlooks the ocean, craftsman-style architecture.
✉ 11480 North Torrey Pines Road ☎ 858/453 4420

The Rest of California

Big Bear Lake

⚜⚜⚜Apples Bed & Breakfast Inn ($$)
A secluded setting close to shops and recreation. Afternoon cider and appertizers.
✉ 42439 Moonridge Road
☎ 909/866 0903

Big Sur

⚜⚜⚜Ventana Inn ($$$)
Luxurious hideaway, comprises 59 separate bungalows. Sweeping views of the coastline.
✉ California Highway 1
☎ 831/667 2331

Carmel

⚜⚜⚜Sandpiper Inn ($$)
Early California inn built in 1929. Some rooms with ocean views.
✉ 2408 Bay View Avenue
☎ 831/624 6433

⚜⚜ ⚜⚜Tickle Pink Inn at Carmel Highlands ($$$)
Coastline views from secluded cottages and rooms. Nonchalant luxury. Afternoon wine and cheese service.
✉ 155 Highland Drive
☎ 831/624 1244

Catalina Island
Hotel Metropole ($$$)
Magnificent ocean views from the rooftop sun deck and spa. In Metropole Marketplace.
✉ **205 Crescent Avenue, Avalon** ☎ **310/510 1884**

Hotel Vista Del Mar ($$)
Resort hotel overlooking beach with larger, comfortable rooms; most with spectacular views.
✉ **417 Crescent Avenue, Avalon** ☎ **310/510 1452**

Death Valley
Furnace Creek Inn ($$$)
Native American décor, built in the 1920s. Choose between regular motel-style rooms and furnished cabins.
✉ **About 1 mile (1.6km) south on CA 190** ☎ **760/786 2345**
🕐 **Oct–May only**

Eureka
Best Western Humboldt Bay Inn ($)
Recently remodeled lodging near Humboldt State Park.
✉ **232 W 5th Street**
☎ **707/443 2234**

Half Moon Bay
The Beach House ($$$)
Large rooms with ocean views, fireplaces like an old New England summer home. Jacuzzis, saunas.
✉ **6 miles (10km) north of Half Moon Bay, 4100 Coast Highway 1** ☎ **650/712 0220**

Lake Arrowhead
Lake Arrowhead Resort ($$)
On the lake in Arrowhead Village. All rooms face the lakefront. Fishing, boating, children's activities.
✉ **27984 Highway 189**
☎ **909/336 1511**

Lake Tahoe
Best Western Station House Inn ($$)
Central to the lake, with great sporting activities. Close to the border casinos.
✉ **901 Park Avenue, South Lake Tahoe** ☎ **530/542 1101**

Mammoth Lakes
Mammoth Mountain Inn ($$$)
Resort complex; free transportation to the ski areas. Horseback riding and hiking/hunting trails are on offer.
✉ **1 Minaret Road** ☎ **760/934 2581**

Mendocino
Headlands Inn ($$)
Remodeled 1868 Victorian with six rooms and one private cottage.
✉ **Howard and Albion streets**
☎ **707/937 4431**

Monterey
Old Monterey Inn ($$$)
English country hotel boasting acres of gardens and spectacular views of Monterey Bay.
✉ **500 Martin Street**
☎ **831/375 8284**

Morro Bay
Best Western El Rancho ($)
Unique redwood lobby. Very reasonable rates.
✉ **2460 Main Street**
☎ **800/628 3500**

Mount Shasta
Tree House Best Western ($$)
Terrific views of the

Bed-and-Breakfast
A recent trend in lodging is the popularity of the bed-and-breakfast and the country inn. Many of these are found in Northern California and Wine Country regions. Many of those who live in the major cities look forward to a weekend in the country at one of these small inns (usually only 10 to 20 rooms). Reservations are difficult to get on the weekends and in the summer, so reserve well in advance.

Motels

For those on a tight budget, it's possible to find a decent motel room (double occupancy) for under $50. Most offer in-room phones, cable television and a pool. There are many motel "chains" that offer safe, clean, reasonably priced lodging for those in transit. Some to look for are Motel 6, Econolodge and Quality Inn.

mountain and excellent skiing in the winter.

✉ Lake Street just off the I–5
☎ 530/926 3101

Ojai

🏵🏵🏵 🏵🏵🏵 Ojai Valley Inn ($$$)
Plush rural surroundings. 220 acres (89ha) that include a championship golf course.
✉ 905 Country Club Road
☎ 805/646 5511

Orange County

🏵🏵🏵 🏵🏵🏵 Four Seasons Hotel ($$$)
One of the finest hotels in the state. Modern design with tree-lined swimming pool and tennis courts.
✉ 690 Newport Center Drive, Newport Beach ☎ 949/759 0808

🏵🏵 🏵🏵 Hilton Waterfront Beach Resort ($$$)
Large resort with beach access, watersports, dining and shopping. Ocean views.
✉ 21100 Pacific Coast Highway, Huntington Beach ☎ 714/845 8000

🏵 🏵 Hotel Laguna ($$)
Affordable and funky, with private beach for guests.
✉ 425 S Coast Highway, Laguna Beach ☎ 949/494 1151

🏵🏵 🏵🏵 Surf and Sand Hotel ($$)
Tasteful, elegant hotel on the beach, near the galleries, shops and restaurants. All rooms with ocean views.
✉ 1555 S Coast Highway, Laguna Beach ☎ 949/497 4477

Palm Springs

🏵🏵 The Inn at Deep Canyon ($–$$)
Basic accommodations in

Palm Desert; some rooms have kitchenettes.
✉ 74–470 Abronia Trail
☎ 760/346 8061

🏵🏵🏵 🏵🏵🏵 La Mancha Private Villas ($$–$$$)
Two or three bedroomed suites, pools, spas, tennis.
✉ 400 N Avenida Caballeros
☎ 760/320 0398

🏵🏵 🏵🏵 Marriott's Desert Springs Resort and Spa ($$$)
Marriott's landmark hotel features an atrium lobby, landscaped gardens, Bob Hope Cultural Center, golf, tennis, man-made beach and an exclusive mall.
✉ 74855 Country Club Drive, Palm Desert ☎ 760/341 2211

Two Bunch Palms Inn ($$$)
Secluded cottages on 300 acres. Natural hot springs, a lake and wooded paths.
✉ 67425 Two Bunch Palms Trail, Desert Hot Springs
☎ 760/329 8791

Pebble Beach

🏵🏵 🏵🏵 The Lodge at Pebble Beach ($$$)
The epitome of opulence. Overlooks Carmel Bay and the world-famous Pebble Beach golf course.
✉ 1700 17-mile Drive, 3 miles (5km) north of Carmel
☎ 831/647 7500

Pismo Beach

🏵🏵 Sea Gypsy Motel ($)
Affordable lodging on the beach.
✉ 1020 Cypress ☎ 805/773 1801

Redwood Forest

🏵🏵 🏵🏵 Benbow Inn ($$$)
Mansion built in 1926.

✉ 445 Lake Benbow Drive, Garberville ☎ 707/923 2124
🕒 Closed Jan–Mar

Sacramento
▽▽▽ ▽▽▽Hyatt Regency ($$)
Located downtown, near the Capitol Building.
✉ 1209 "L" Street ☎ 916/443 1234

San Luis Obispo
Apple Farm Inn ($$)
A quaint inn complete with working millhouse and bakery.
✉ 2015 Monterey Street
☎ 805/544 2040

Santa Barbara
▽▽▽Montecito Inn ($$$)
This inn was built in 1928 by Charlie Chaplin and Fatty Arbuckle; the inn takes its facilities and service quite seriously.
✉ 1295 Coast Village Road
☎ 805/969 7854

Santa Cruz
▽▽▽Sea and Sand Inn ($$)
Budget hotel, overlooking the cliffs.
✉ 201 W Cliff Drive
☎ 831/427 3400

Solvang
▽▽Solvang Royal Scandinavian Inn ($$)
Decorated attractively in Scandinavian style. Centrally located for Solvang's attractions.
✉ 400 Alisal Road ☎ 805/688 8000

▽▽▽Storybook Inn ($$)
European-style inn offers a retreat-like ambience in the center of town.
✉ 409 First Street ☎ 805/688 1703

Wine Country
▽▽▽ ▽▽▽Foothill House ($$$)
Charmingly remodeled, turn-of-the-century farmhouse.
✉ 3037 Foothill Boulevard, Calistoga ☎ 707/942 6933

▽▽▽ ▽▽▽Harvest Inn ($$$)
Small English Tudor inn surrounded by vineyards. Many rooms have fireplaces and antique furnishings.
✉ One Main Street, St. Helena
☎ 707/963 9463

▽▽▽Napa Inn ($$)
Romantic, turn-of-the-century Queen Anne Victorian. In downtown Napa near shops and restaurants.
✉ 1137 Warren Street, Napa
☎ 707/257 1444

▽▽▽ ▽▽▽Silverado Resort ($$$)
Large resort with wine tastings and sport facilities.
✉ 1600 Atlas Peak Road, Napa
☎ 707/257 0200

▽▽▽Sonoma Mission Inn and Spa ($$$)
Exclusive spa in the Spanish-mission style.
✉ Sonoma Highway, Sonoma
☎ 707/938 9000

▽▽▽Trojan Horse Inn ($$)
Only six rooms in this restored frontier home.
✉ 19455 Sonoma Highway, Sonoma ☎ 707/996 2430

Yosemite
▽▽▽ ▽▽▽Tenaya Lodge at Yosemite ($$)
Rustic riverside elegance, cookouts and wagon rides.
✉ 2 miles (3.2km) south of the park's south gate ☎ 559/683 6555

Campgrounds
An alternative to hotels and motels are the state's many campgrounds. Most of the state and national parks have campgrounds that offer tent or RV sites, outdoor cooking areas, public rest rooms and shower facilities. The fee is usually under $10 per night. Private campgrounds adjacent to the parks offer additional facilities at a slightly higher rate. June through September is a busy time.

Art & Antiques/ Fashion/Crafts/Stores

Popular Shopping Venues

San Francisco and Los Angeles are the two most popular shopping areas in California. From large, multi-level shopping centers to streets filled with discount and specialty shops, you can find just about anything your heart desires. Included here are just a few of the most popular areas to get you started. Check the local newspapers, especially on Sunday, for sales and discounts.

Art & Antiques

San Francisco
Fillmore Street
Specialty shops include book and music stores, and clothing from retro to new fashion.
✉ **Jackson & Sutter**

The Japan Center
Art galleries and Oriental gift shops, interspersed with sushi bars and tea houses.
✉ **Bounded by Laguna, Geary, Fillmore, Sutter and Post streets**

Los Angeles
La Cienega Boulevard south of Santa Monica Boulevard, Beverly Boulevard west of the Beverly Center, Melrose Avenue in Hollywood, and Santa Monica's Third Street Promenade are all lined with excellent, but costly antiques stores and art galleries.

San Diego
Antique Row
More than 20 dealers give this street its name.
✉ **Adams Avenue, Kensington**

The Olde Cracker Factory
Antiques center of the area.
✉ **448 W Market** ☎ **619/233 1669**

Rest Of California

Mendocino
This small town in northern California is considered the artistic center of the North Coast.

Mendocino Arts Center
Two art galleries, along with numerous arts and crafts fairs.
✉ **45200 Little Lake Street** ☎ **707/937 5818 and 800/653 3328**

Santa Rosa (Wine Country)
Railroad Square
A historic square featuring antiques stores, curio shops.
☎ **707/578 8478**

Fashion

San Francisco
Haight Street
Famous for hippies in the 1960s; some shops still sell offbeat, vintage clothes. Book and music shops.
✉ **At Ashbury Street**

SoMa
Popular for bargain stores, night-spots and cafés.
✉ **South of Market Street**

Union Square
Large department stores are Macy's, Neiman-Marcus and Saks Fifth Avenue.
✉ **Downtown** ☎ **Macy's 415/397 3333; Neiman-Marcus 415/362 3900; Saks Fifth Avenue 415/986 4300**

Union Street
One of the best streets in San Francisco, with specialist shops/galleries.
✉ **Between Gough and Steiner**

Los Angeles
Garment District
Fashion bargains in open store fronts and inside the huge Cooper Building. Stroll through the California Mart to see upcoming fashions.
✉ **Los Angeles Street and 7th Street, Downtown**

Melrose Avenue
Three-mile (5km) strip of shops from Aardvark's used clothing, to vintage stores and upscale boutiques.
✉ **Between Highland and Doheny, Hollywood**

Rodeo Drive
Renowned as being the most exclusive and expensive shopping area on the West Coast. Top designer clothes and accessories.

✉ **Between Santa Monica and Wilshire boulevards, Beverly Hills**

Venice Beach
Unique and amazingly inexpensive sunwear and hip formal dress.

✉ **Oceanfront Walk, Venice**

San Diego
The Paladion
Posh center with Cartier, Tiffany's, Gucci and more.

✉ **Across from Horton Plaza**

Rest of California

Palm Springs
El Paseo
Exclusive shops that rival Beverly Hills Rodeo Drive. Art galleries.

✉ **Visitors Center, 2901 N Palm Canyon Drive** ☎ **760/778 8418**

Crafts

San Francisco
Fisherman's Wharf
There are four shopping centers here—Pier 39, The Cannery, Ghirardelli Square and The Anchorage.

✉ **Columbus on the Bay**

Los Angeles
Olvera Street
Mexican crafts and gifts, clothing and cafés on LA's oldest street.

✉ **Los Angeles Street**

San Diego
Gaslamp Quarter
A must for the arts and crafts crowd. The Quarter takes in 38 acres (15ha) in the National Historic District.

✉ **Fifth Avenue from Broadway to the waterfront**

Stores

San Francisco
The Embarcadero Center
Shops, restaurants, offices, hotels in a huge downtown complex.

✉ **Sacramento and Clay streets** 🚇 **BART, Muni**

Ghirardelli Square
Formerly a chocolate factory, this area has become a chic center of stores and top restaurants.

✉ **At Fisherman's Wharf**

Los Angeles
Beverly Center
Three-tiered upscale mall, with exterior elevators that offer a great view of the area. Macy's, Broadway, Bullocks, Hard Rock Café.

✉ **Beverly Boulevard and La Cienega, Beverly Hills**

Century City
Features international food court with indoor/outdoor dining, theater, fine dining, Bloomingdale's. Macey's.

✉ **10250 Santa Monica Boulevard, Beverly Hills**

Westside Pavilion
Multi-level with modern, open-air atrium; Nordstrom, Robinsons-May and others.

✉ **Pico and Westwood boulevards**

San Diego
Fashion Valley Mall
This and Mission Valley are the city's two main shopping centres. Six major department stores.

✉ **352 Fashion Valley Road**

Tijuana
Shoppers in San Diego often find themselves drawn to Tijuana, just across the California–Mexico border. The Free-Port status makes for great bargains. Prices are reasonable, and haggling is welcomed as part of the fun. The best shopping areas are the mall at Agua Caliente Race Track and the Avenida Revolución, the city's oldest tourist shopping area. Take precautions with your valuables when traveling across the border.

Factory Outlets/ Produce/Gifts

Outlet and Factory Stores
The latest US shopping trend is outlet and factory stores. Don't be fooled by these "malls," however, as many of the shops rival the parent stores in pricing. Although you have to look carefully, there are enough bargains on the name-brand items to warrant the outlets' popularity. Along the same lines are huge indoor and outdoor flea markets and "swap meets" that offer both new and used items.

Rest of California

Monterey
Cannery Row
Unique shops and restaurants line this nautical area, made famous by John Steinbeck's novel *Cannery Row*.
✉ **Fisherman's Wharf**

Orange County
South Coast Plaza
This is Orange County's largest and most exclusive mall, with three huge sections connected by free tram. All major department stores are located within this complex, along with a wide variety of specialty stores.

Factory Outlets

Folsom
Folsom Factory Store
The 50 stores here include names like Nike, Jones NY, Bass.
✉ **13000 Folsom**

Gilroy
Outlets at Gilroy
More than 100 stores. Includes Gap, Ann Taylor, Espirit among others.
✉ **681 Leavesley**

Lake Elsinore
Lake Elsinore Outlet Center
Van Huesen and Levi's are just two of the 70 stores located here.
✉ **17600 Collier Avenue**

Mammoth Lakes
Mammoth Factory Store
Only 10 stores, but they are some of the best, with names like Ralph Lauren, and Bass.
✉ **3343 Main Street**

Monterey
American Tin Cannery Factory Outlet
Izod and Nine West are just two of the nearly 40 stores.
✉ **125 Ocean View Boulevard, Pacific Grove**

Petaluma
Petaluma Village Factory Outlet
Fifty stores from Saks to Coach to Gap.
✉ **2200 Petaluma Boulevard**

Pismo Beach
Pismo Beach Outlet Center
Jones New York, Bass, Mikasa, Levi's; 40 shops in all.
✉ **333 5-Cities Drive**

Solvang
Solvang Outlet Stores
Small but élite, featuring Donna Karen, Ellen Tracy, Brooks Bros.
✉ **3202 N Alisal Road**

Wine Country
Napa Factory Store
Liz Claiborne, J. Crew, Tommy Hilfiger; 50 in all.
✉ **629 Factory Street Drive, Napa**

Produce

San Francisco
Chinatown
Almost as fun as finding unique produce and great bargains is watching the locals wrangle for better prices.
✉ **Bordered by Broadway, Bush, Kearny and Powell streets**

Los Angeles
Farmers Market
Over 100 sellers of not only fresh produce but gifts, food and clothes, all at affordable

prices. Open-air cafés
(►49).

✉ **Third and Fairfax,
Hollywood**

Gifts

San Francisco
Chinatown
Asian specialty shops, fresh
produce, and incredible
architecture (►35).

✉ **Bordered by Broadway,
Bush, Kearny & Powell streets**

Fisherman's Wharf
Street performers entertain
as you explore the 100
shops and restaurants
clustered around the piers
(►36).

✉ **Between The Embarcadero
and Columbus Avenue**

Los Angeles
Hollywood Boulevard
The place to go to find rare
movie memorabilia and
posters. Theaters and restaurants for every mood and
budget.

✉ **Between La Brea and
Highland**

Little Tokyo
Unusual Oriental items.
Outdoor shopping/dining.

✉ **San Pedro & First streets,
Downtown**

Venice Beach
Outdoor booths with great
prices, if you aren't
distracted by the street
artists and Muscle Beach
iron-pumpers.

✉ **Oceanfront between
Washington & Santa Monica
Boulevards**

San Diego
Old Town
Small gift boutiques and
cafés among flower gardens,

fountains and courtyards in
the style of a Mexican
marketplace. One of the best
antiques shopping areas in
Southern California. Bargain
prices for valuable items at
local antiques shops.

✉ **Mason Street and San
Diego Avenue**

Rest of California

Monterey Bay
Peter Rabbit and Friends
Toys, music boxes and
clothing featuring some of
the characters and scenes
from Beatrix Potter's
children's stories.

✉ **Lincoln Avenue between
7th and Ocean avenues**
☎ **831/624 6854**

Sacramento
David Berkeley's
Eclectic variations from
extensive wine selections
by White House wine
consultant, David Berkeley,
to Epicurean European
foods and country-flavored
gifts.

✉ **515 Pavillions Lane**
☎ **916/929 4422**

Wine Country
**All Seasons Cafe Wine
Shop**
A selection of the best of the
hundreds of wine shops in
Napa Valley. Most sell gifts
and other unique products,
and will ship anywhere in the
world.

✉ **1400 Lincoln Avenue,
Calistoga** ☎ **707/942 9111**

Shaker Shops West
Quality reproductions of
Shaker furniture and gifts,
deep in California's north
country.

✉ **5 Inverness Way, Inverness**
☎ **415/669 7256**

Farmers' Markets
Almost every city and
town in California has an
open-air or farmers'
market, and roadside
stands dot country roads
and state highways.
These markets are great
places to find unique gifts
or cherished mementoes
of your visit, and their
prices are generally lower
than more urban retailers.
Whatever type of
shopping you prefer,
locals residents are happy
to point you to the most
popular shopping places.

Children's Attractions

Avoid the Long Lines
Most of the larger California cities have fine museums that are inexpensive and provide interactive exhibits. A hint for avoiding long lines at theme parks is to arrive early, or just an hour or two before closing.

San Francisco
Children's Fairyland
This inexpensive 10-acre (4-ha) park, with exhibits from nursery rhymes, is said to have intrigued Walt Disney so much he built Disneyland Park to copy it.
✉ 699 Bellevue Avenue ☎ 510/238 6876 🕐 Fri–Sun 10–4; extended hours in summer

Paramount's Great America
The Bay area's place for roller coasters and other daredevil rides. Fort-Fun is an interactive parent/child area. Top Gun and Smurf Woods rides are the most popular. Also features stage shows, musicals, puppet shows and wildlife shows.
✉ Great American Parkway, Santa Clara (about 45 miles/73km south of San Francisco) ☎ 408/988 1776 🕐 Sat, Sun 10–7; weekdays summer only

Raging Waters
The Bay area's only water theme park, with large and long waterslides designed to please. There are over 30 different attractions. Older children will love the innertube rides.
✉ Lake Cunningham Park, San Jose ☎ 408/238 9900 🕐 May–Sep, call for hours

Santa Cruz Beach Boardwalk
This historical landmark, dating to 1907, was the first full-scale amusement park on the West Coast. With roller-coasters and haunted castles, bumper cars and a ferris wheel, this is an "oldie but goodie."
✉ 400 Beach Street, Santa Cruz ☎ 831/423 5590 🕐 Call for hours

Los Angeles
Disneyland Park (▶ 18)

Hollywood Guinness World of Records
Trivia galore from The-Animal-with-The-Smallest-Brain-in-Proportion-to-Body-Size (a Stegosaurus) to The Most Biographed Female (Marilyn Monroe).
✉ 6764 Hollywood Boulevard, Hollywood ☎ 323/463 6433 🕐 Daily 10am–11pm 💵 Moderate

Hollywood Wax Museum (▶ 51)

Knott's Berry Farm (▶ 78)

The Pacific Ocean
The whole family can frolic on one of the many beaches that line the Pacific Ocean. Venice offers bicycle, skateboard and stroller rentals and playgrounds; the Pier at Santa Monica has rides, including the indoor carousel seen in the movie *The Sting*, arcades and shops; Malibu Beach is home to many celebrities. Further north on Pacific Coast Highway are more sandy beaches for sunning, swimming and surfing (like Leo Carillo, Zuma, Monterey Presidio), and there are even campgrounds right on the beach for a minimum cost. Summer reservations a must.

Universal Studios (▶ 54)

San Diego
Balboa Park (▶ 16)

Legoland California
This Danish import opened in 1999, and the entire park is built out of lego pieces.

Rides and exhibits are usually packed.

✉ 1 Lego Drive, Carlsbad
☎ 760/918 5346 🕓 Call for hours 💷 Expensive

San Diego Zoo (▶ 16)
☎ 619/234 3153 🕓 Daily 9–4; zoo grounds close at 6pm
💷 Inexpensive

Sea World (▶ 64)

Rest of California

La Habra
Children's Museum at La Habra
Restored railroad station exhibiting a wide range of scientific and historical artifacts. Special events and programs.

✉ 301 Euclid Street, La Habra
☎ 562/905 9793 🕓 Mon 10–1, Tue–Sat 10–5, Sun 1–5
💷 Inexpensive

Lake Arrowhead
Lake Arrowhead Children's Museum
Contains historical information on the area and anthropological exhibitions. Kids can pretend they are ants in a life-size colony.

✉ Lake Arrowhead Village
☎ 909/336 3093 🕓 Daily 10–5, 10–6 in summer 💷 Inexpensive

Paso Robles
Atascadero Lake Park and Charles Paddock Zoo
Intimate zoo with jaguars from Brazil, Bengal tigers, pink flamingos and lots of chimps. Nominal entry fee. Next to the zoo is a beautiful lake with picnic facilities.

✉ State Route 41, south of Paso Robles ☎ 805/461 5080
🕓 Zoo: daily 10–4, 10–5 in summer. Lake Park: daily until sundown

Lake Nacimiento Resort
One of the most popular family resorts in the state. Great outdoor activities, including fishing and diving. Features a full-service marina and dock where you can rent anything from jet-skis to pontoon boats. Lodge, camp-grounds and RV facilities.

✉ County Road G–14 out of Paso Robles ☎ 805/238 3256 🕓 Daily to sundown

Sacramento
Six Flags Waterworld
This park has some of the best high-speed slides and other water attractions.

✉ Exposition Boulevard
☎ 916/924 0556 🕓 Late May–early Sep; call for hours
💷 Expensive

Santa Ana
Kidseum
Kids won't even realize they're being educated about world cultures as they take part in the storytelling, puppet shows and other exhibits at this interactive museum.

✉ 1802 Main Street ☎ 714/567 3600 (Bowes Museum and College of Art) 🕓 Summer Tue–Sun noon–4; winter Sat–Sun 11–4

Valencia
Six Flags Magic Mountain
Specializing in thrill rides, the park also offers a mini-zoo and the Wizard's Village for the younger members of the family. Admission price covers everything but food, including puppet shows, dance revues and other live entertainment.

✉ 26101 Magic Mountain Parkway, off Interstate 5 Freeway ☎ 661/255 4103
🕓 Call for hours

Pacifying the Kids
For enjoyable travel with children, don't overdo it. Adult stress reflects in youngsters. Kids love to help plan excursions and navigate from the map, and allowing them to do so teaches valuable skills. To avoid grouchy kids and frazzled adults, take frequent breaks, especially on long road trips. And most importantly, see the sights through their eyes for a unique perspective often lost in the grown-up world.

Museums/Concert Halls/Nightlife

TV and Film
California's film industry means major cities teem with movie theaters. Check local papers for listings or pick up a free *LA* or *San Francisco Weekly* at restaurants, shops. For variation, there's the Silent Movie theater (Hollywood), the alternative Red Vic Movie House (Haight), the live vaudevillian Fabulous Palm Springs Follies (☎ 760/327 0225), or join a television studio audience (☎ 818/506 0043).

Museums

San Francisco
Exploratorium/Palace of Fine Arts
Crème de la crème of science museums. Exhibits of art, science and human perception. The Tactile Dome is wonderful.
⊠ 3601 Lyon Street
☎ 415/561 0360 🕐 Tue–Sun 10–5, Mon, hols 10–5, Memorial Day–Labor Day daily 10–6

SFMOMA (▶ 39)
⊠ 151 Third Street
☎ 415/357 4000 🕐 Mon, Tue, Fri–Sun 11–5.45, Thu 11–8.45; closed Wed 🛡 Free 1st Tue of month

Los Angeles
Armand Hammer Museum of Art and Cultural Center
Holds the largest US collection of French artist Honoré Dumier.
⊠ 10899 Wilshire Westwood
☎ 310/443 7000 🕐 Tue, Wed, Fri, Sat 11–7, Thu 11–9, Sun 11–5

California Museum of Science & Industry (▶ 50)
⊠ 700 State Drive, Exposition Park ☎ 323/724 3623
🕐 Daily 10–5

Huntington Library, Art Gallery and Botanical Gardens (▶ 52)
⊠ 1151 Oxford Road, San Marino ☎ 626/405 2141

Museum of Contemporary Art (MOCA) (▶ 53)
⊠ 250 S Grand Avenue
☎ 213/626 6222

Museum of Tolerance
Interactive exhibits of hate activities (Holocaust, riots) designed to promote understanding.

⊠ 9786 W Pico ☎ 310/553 8403 🕐 Mon–Thu 11.30–4, Fri 11.30–3 (1pm Nov–Mar), Sun 11–5 🛡 Moderate

Rest of California

Monterey
Pacific House
Old West hotel and saloon-turned-museum.
⊠ 10 Custom House Plaza
☎ 831/649 7118 🕐 Tue–Sun 10–4

Sacramento
Crocker Art Museum
Oldest art museum in the American West. European, Asian and California art in 19th-century building.
⊠ 216 "O" Street ☎ 916/264 5423 🕐 Tue–Sun 10–5, Thu 10–9

Concert Halls

San Francisco
Louise M. Davies Symphony Hall
Symphonies, concerts; also tours of this stream-lined glass-and-granite building.
⊠ Van Ness Avenue and Grove Street, Civic Center ☎ 415/864 6000

Los Angeles
Hollywood Bowl
Outdoor arena, year-round headline concerts of every music style, especially the LA Philharmonic.
⊠ 2301 N Highland Avenue, Hollywood ☎ 323/850 2000

Wiltern Theatre
Intimate, acoustically wonderful hall that features top-name musical performances in the art deco Wiltern Center.
⊠ Wilshire and Western
☎ 213/480 3232

San Diego
Civic Theatre
Ultramodern design provides a great backdrop to concerts held here.

📧 San Diego Concourse, 202 "C" Street ☎ 619/615 4100

Nightlife

San Francisco
Bottom of the Hill
Alternative bands head to this Potrero Hill club, which has a beer garden, pool tables and also serves food.

📧 1233 17th Street ☎ 415/621 4455 (information line)

111 Minna
An art gallery that does double duty as a DJ/dance venue in the evenings.

📧 111 Minna Street, at 2nd Street ☎ 415/974 1719

Vesuvio Cafe
This former haunt of Beat poets hasn't changed much in 30 years.

📧 255 Columbus Avenue ☎ 415/362 3370

Los Angeles
The Baked Potato
Oldest major contemporary jazz club in California. Big-name entertainment for a moderate cost.

📧 3787 Cahuenga Boulevard W, North Hollywood ☎ 818/980 1615

Bar Marmont
Intimate French colonial café, usually full of celebrities and paparazzi.

📧 6171 Sunset Boulevard, Hollywood ☎ 323/650 0575

BB King's Blues Club
Three floors. Lucille's room is acoustic on Fri and Sat.

📧 1000 Universal City Drive, Universal City ☎ 818/622 5464

Cat & Fiddle Pub and Restaurant
Ambient outdoor patio. Sunday jazz jam. No cover.

📧 6530 Sunset Boulevard, Hollywood ☎ 323/468 3800

Cowboy Palace Saloon
The last real honky tonk in California. Live country seven nights. Pool, darts, dance classes. No cover.

📧 21635 Devonshire Street, Chatsworth ☎ 818/341 0166

Good Luck Bar
Knocked out of the No. 1 spot by Bar Marmont, but now you finally have room to dance and enjoy yourself.

📧 1514 Hillhurst Avenue, Los Feliz ☎ 323/666 3524

The Improvisation (Improv)
See the place where many comedians got their start.

📧 8162 Melrose, West Hollywood ☎ 323/651 2583

Molly Malone's Irish Pub
Small neighborhood bar with Irish folk, rock & roll, R & B nightly. Cover varies.

📧 575 S Fairfax ☎ 323/935 1577

Rage
Gay/lesbian meeting place, alternative/underground music.

📧 8911 Santa Monica Boulevard, West Hollywood ☎ 310/652 7055

San Diego
Top O' the Cove
Piano bar/restaurant featuring show tunes and standards.

📧 1216 Prospect Street, La Jolla ☎ 858/454 7779

Out on the Town
Karaoke's hot, but there's no lack of other choices for night-time entertainment in California: headline concerts to acoustical folk by local solo artists, poetry-readings to comedy, dramatic plays and musicals to raunchy revues. Even in the small communities, you can find live entertainment, with country music being the most popular. Parking can be difficult in Los Angeles, but valet parking is available at a reasonable cost.

Nightlife/Performing Arts Theaters/Sports

Pro Sports

For those who would rather watch than participate, pro sports are abundant in the state. Besides pro golf tours, there are several renowned horse-racing parks, especially Del Mar, a beachside track just north of San Diego. San Diego has pro baseball and football; LA has Clippers and Lakers basketball, baseball and hockey; San Diego has baseball, football, soccer and ice hockey. The Bay Area has pro baseball, football, basketball and hockey. Information can be obtained from team offices. College sports add elan to the mix.

Nightlife

Rest of California

Eureka
Lost Coast Brewery & Café
Microbreweries are the rage, and this is one of the best.
✉ 617 Fourth Street
☎ 707/445 4480

Sacramento
Harlow's
Most glamorous nightclub in town. Upstairs is Momo's cigar lounge.
✉ 2708 "J" Street ☎ 916/441 4693

The Monkey Bar
Favorite haunt of the hip. Arrive early if you want to sit.
✉ 2730 Capitol Avenue
☎ 916/442 8490

Sacramento Brewing Company's Oasis
Locally produced, award-winning beer.
✉ 7811 Capitol Avenue
☎ 916/966 6274

Performing Arts/ Theaters

San Francisco
Orpheum Theatre
The largest touring shows to San Francisco play here.
✉ 1192 Market Street
☎ 415/551 2000

American Conservatory Theater (ACT)
One of the top regional theaters in the US.
✉ 415 Geary Street
☎ 415/749 2228

Los Angeles
Music Center of Los Angeles County
Includes Dorothy Chandler Pavilion, Mark Taper Forum, featuring experiment plays; the Ahmanson, with musical comedies and the Walt Disney Concert Hall.
✉ 135 N Grand, downtown
☎ 213/972 7211

San Diego
Lawrence Welk Resort Theatre
Dinner theater, with Broadway and Broadway-style shows. Buffet matinee and evening.
✉ 8860 Lawrence Welk Drive, Escondido ☎ 760/749 3448

Sledgehammer Theatre
Avant-garde productions.
✉ 1620 Sixth Avenue
☎ 619/544 1484

Rest of California

Orange County
Orange County Performing Arts Center
Regular performances by New York City Opera, American Ballet Theater and Los Angeles Philharmonic Orchestra, plus present-ations of popular musicals.
✉ 600 Town Center Drive, Costa Mesa ☎ 714/556 2787

Spectator Sports

Los Angeles
Los Angeles Galaxy
The Los Angeles soccer team play at the Home Depot Center.
✉ 18400 Avalon Boulevard, Carson ☎ 310/630 2200

Indio
Eldorado Polo Club
The "Winter Polo Capital of the West." Weekday practice matches are free. Picnic grounds.
✉ 50–950 Madison Street
☎ 760/342 2223

Monterey
Mazda Raceway Laguna Seca
Four major auto races a year, including restored antique cars.
✉ 1021 Monterey Road, Salinas 93908 ☎ 831/648 5100

Sports

San Francisco
Several companies along the wharf offer sailing, fishing excursions and boat rentals. Some off-pier fishing as well.

Los Angeles
Moonlight Rollerway
Moonlight is one of the more popular indoor roller-blading rinks in LA.
✉ 5110 San Fernando Road, Glendale ☎ 818/241 3630

Pershing Square
The outdoor ice rink opens in November.
✉ Pershing Square Station on Metro Red Line ☎ 818/243 6488

Santa Anita Race Track
Bet on horses during the track's season, from December to April.
✉ 285 West Huntington Drive ☎ 626/574 7223 🕐 Dec 26–late Apr

Sports Center Bowl
The landmark Jerry's Deli is right next door for a snack, after you've worked up an appetite.
✉ 12655 Ventura Boulevard, Studio City ☎ 818/769 7600
🕐 Call for open bowling hours

Rest of California

Lake Tahoe
Ski Lake Tahoe Association
Package deals available on the 15 downhill and 11 cross-country ski areas. Free shuttle between all.
☎ 888/824 6338 (Snow Ski); 530/544 7747 (Water Ski School)

Monterey
Monterey Bay Kayaks
Kayak rentals, tours.
✉ 693 Del Monte Avenue ☎ 831/373 5357

Palm Springs
Mission Hills Resort Golf Club
One reason Palm Springs is "Winter Golf Capital of the World."
✉ 71–501 Dinah Shore Drive, Rancho Mirage ☎ 760/328 3198

Palm Springs Tennis Center
Nine lighted courts open to the public.
✉ 1300 Baristo Road ☎ 760/320 0020

Pebble Beach
Spyglass Hill
Less expensive than Pebble Beach course (which hosts the AT&T ProAm tour), the bordering Pacific and Del Monte Forest make this difficult but scenic. Reserve a month in advance (year for groups).
✉ Spyglass Hill Road ☎ 831/624 3811

Solvang
Windhaven Glider
Breathtaking glider rides.
✉ Santa Ynez Airport ☎ 805/688 2517 🕐 10–5 daily

Yosemite
Try rock-climbing, backpacking, camping, and hiking, guided or not. Sheer El Capitan mountain, at 3,500ft (1067m), attracts world-class climbers in search of a challenge.

Choices
California offers the unique opportunity to visit multiple environments, all within a 24-hour period. You can spend the morning backpacking in the desert, the afternoon riding horses on wooded mountain trails, then head for the ocean for clam-digging or shell-hunting, and a sail into the sunset. For something different, cruise over to Mexico for some fast-paced jai alai (Fronton Palacio, ☎ 619/298 4105).

What's On When

The following are just a few of California's myriad festivals and celebrations.

January
Tournament of Roses Parade, Pasadena
Palm Springs International Film Festival

February
Chinese New Year Celebration, San Francisco
Napa Valley Mustard Celebration, Napa

March
International Asian Film Festival, San Francisco
Los Angeles Marathon
Mendocino Whale Festival

April
Toyota Grand Prix, Long Beach
Cherry Blossom Festival, San Francisco
Palm Desert Springfest, Palm Desert
Cinco De Mayo Celebration, state-wide

May
San Francisco International Film Fest
Muscle Car Show, Bakersfield
Sacramento Jazz Jubilee
San Francisco Bay to Breakers, a race where people run in costume

June
Scottish Highlands Games and Gathering of the Clans, Modesto
Amador County Wine Festival, Plymouth
Sonoma Valley Shakespeare Festival, Sonoma

July
Festival of Arts and Pageant of the Masters, Laguna Beach
California Rodeo, Salinas
Greek Festival, Santa Barbara
San Francisco Marathon

August
Mozart Festival, San Luis Obispo
Sawdust Festival, Laguna Beach
San Francisco Mime Troupe Summer Park Season
Old Spanish Days Fiesta, Santa Barbara
Japanese Cultural Bazaar, Sacramento
California State Fair, Sacramento
Children's Festival of the Arts, Hollywood

September
Greek Food Festival, Sacramento
Oktoberfest, Huntington Beach
Danish Days, Solvang
Monterey Jazz Festival, Monterey
Armenian Food Festival, San Francisco
Bowlful of Blues Festival, Ojai
California International Air Show, Salinas

October
Jazz Festival, San Francisco
Rose Show, Santa Barbara
San Francisco Fleet week

November
West Coast Ragtime Festival, in various locations
Christmas Parade, Hollywood

December
America's Tallest Living Christmas Tree, Ferndale
Newport Harbor Christmas Boat Parade, Newport Beach
Celebrity Cooks and Kitchens Tour, Mendocino

Practical Matters

Above: T-shirts at
Venice Beach
Right: Having fun
on the Boardwalk
at Santa Cruz, a
traditional
American seaside
resort

TIME DIFFERENCES

GMT	California	Germany	USA (NY)	Netherlands	Spain
12 noon	← 4am	→ 1pm	← 7am	→ 1pm	→ 1pm

BEFORE YOU GO

WHAT YOU NEED

● Required
○ Suggested
▲ Not required

Some countries require a passport to remain valid for a minimum period (usually at least six months) beyond the date of entry—contact their consulate

	UK	Germany	USA	Netherlands	Spain
Passport	●	●	▲	●	●
Visa (regulations can change—check before booking your trip)	▲	▲	▲	▲	▲
Onward or Return Ticket	●	●	▲	●	●
Health Inoculations	▲	▲	▲	▲	▲
Health Documentation (▶ 123, Health)	●	●	●	●	●
Travel Insurance	○	○	○	○	○
Driving Licence (national)	●	●	●	●	●
Car Insurance Certificate (if own car)	○	○	○	○	○

WHEN TO GO

San Francisco

High season

Low season

13°C	14°C	17°C	18°C	19°C	21°C	22°C	22°C	23°C	22°C	18°C	14°C
JAN	FEB	MAR	APR	MAY	JUN	JUL	AUG	SEP	OCT	NOV	DEC

Very wet · Wet · Cloud · Sun

TOURIST OFFICES

In the UK
Visit USA Association
☎ 09069 101020
(consumer line)
www.visitusa.org.uk

In the USA
California Division of
Tourism
801 K Street, Suite 1600,
Sacramento, CA 95812
☎ 916/444 4429,
call-free 800/862 2543;

fax: 916/322 3402
www.visitcalifornia.com

POLICE 911

FIRE 911

AMBULANCE 911

WHEN YOU ARE THERE

ARRIVING

International direct flights operate into Los Angeles (☎ 310/646 5252)—one of the world's busiest airports—and San Francisco (☎ 650/821 8211). San Diego Airport also has international flights but most stop en route first. Charter flights also use these airports.

Los Angeles Airport
Miles to city center

15 miles (24km)

Journey times

🚆 45–60 minutes

🚌 35 minutes

🚗 30 minutes

San Francisco Airport
Miles to city center

16 miles (26km)

Journey times

🚆 N/A

🚌 30–60 minutes

🚗 30 minutes

MONEY

The American monetary unit is the dollar ($), which is divided into 100 cents. There are coins of 1 cent (penny), 5 cents (nickel), 10 cents (dime), 25 cents (quarter), 50 cents (half dollar) and 1 dollar. Notes (bills) are in denominations of 1, 2, 5, 10, 20, 50 and 100 dollars. Be warned, though: all notes, whatever their value, are *exactly the same color (green) and size*.

TIME

 California is on Pacific Standard Time; eight hours behind Greenwich Mean Time (GMT-8), but from early April, when clocks are put forward one hour, to late October, Daylight Saving Time (GMT-7) operates. California is also three hours behind the east coast of the USA (Eastern Standard

CUSTOMS

 YES

Goods Obtained Duty Free for Import into the USA:
Alcohol (spirits): 1L
Cigarettes: 200 *or*
Cigars (not Cuban): 50 *or*
Tobacco: 4.4 pounds (*or* proportionate amounts of each).
Gifts up to the value of $100 (including 100 cigars in addition to the tobacco allowance above); only for non-US residents and may only be claimed once in six months.
(You must be 21 and over to benefit from the alcohol allowance and over 17 for the tobacco allowance.)

 NO

Drugs, firearms, ammunition, offensive weapons, explosives, obscene material, some foods and agricultural items.

CONSULATES

UK	**Germany**	**Netherlands**	**Spain**
310/481 0031 (LA)	323/930 2703 (LA)	310 268 1598 (LA)	323/938 0158 (LA)
	415 775 1061 (SF)		415 922 2995 (SF)

WHEN YOU ARE THERE

TOURIST OFFICES

- Anaheim/ Orange County Visitor & Convention Bureau, 800 West Katella Avenue, Anaheim, CA 92802, ☎ 714/765 8857

- California Deserts Tourism Association, 37–115 Palm View Road, Rancho Mirage, CA 92270, ☎ 760/328 9256

- Los Angeles Convention & Visitors Bureau, 685 Figueroa Street, Los Angeles, CA 90017 ☎ 213/689 8822

- Monterey Peninsula Visitors & Convention Bureau, 150 Oliver Street, PO Box 1770, Monterey, CA 93940, ☎ 831/649 1770

- Palm Springs Tourism, 777 N Canyon Drive, Suite 201, Palm Springs, CA 92264, ☎ 760/778 8415

- Sacramento Convention & Visitors Bureau, 1608 I Street, Sacramento, CA 95814, ☎ 916/264 7777

- San Diego Convention & Visitors Bureau, 401 B Street, Suite 1400, San Diego, CA 92101, ☎ 619/236 1212

- San Francisco Convention & Visitors Bureau, 201 Third Street, Suite 900, San Francisco, CA 94103, ☎ 415/974 6900

NATIONAL HOLIDAYS

J	F	M	A	M	J	J	A	S	O	N	D
2	2			1		1		2	1	2	1

Jan 1	New Year's Day
Jan (3rd Mon)	Martin Luther King Jr's Birthday
Feb 12	Lincoln's Birthday
Feb (3rd Mon)	President's Day
Jul 4	Independence Day
Sep (1st Mon)	Labor Day
Oct (2nd Mon)	Columbus Day
Nov 11	Veteran's Day
Nov (4th Thu)	Thanksgiving Day
Dec 25	Christmas Day

On these days shops, banks and businesses close.

OPENING HOURS

○ Shops	● Attractions/museums
● Offices	● Post offices
● Banks	● Pharmacies

9am	10am	11am	12pm	2pm	3pm	4pm	5pm	6pm

☐ Day	☐ Midday
☐ Evening	

In addition to the times shown above, many shops, particularly department stores within shopping malls, are open evenings and during afternoons on Sunday. Some supermarkets and grocery shops open 24 hours. Banks open until 5.30pm Friday and some major banks open on Saturday. Banks in some major towns and tourist areas may have longer hours. Some pharmacies open from 7am to 9pm or even midnight, while some open 24 hours. Opening times of attractions and museums vary (see individual entries in the What to See section). Some post offices open

**DRIVE ON THE
RIGHT**

**Lavatories
FREE**

PUBLIC TRANSPORT

Internal Flights Flying is the quickest way of getting around California and is not all that expensive if you take advantage of deals offered by airlines. The international airports of San Francisco, Oakland, Los Angeles and San Diego connect with a number of regional airports.

Trains Rail service is provided by America's National Railroad Corporation, Amtrak, which serves 72 California cities and towns. Carriages are clean, comfortable and rarely crowded. A Far Western Region Rail Pass (available only outside the US) gives 45 days unlimited travel over the far Western states.

Long Distance Buses Buses are by far the cheapest way of getting around. Greyhound Lines operates an inter-city service and also links many smaller towns within California. The Ameripass (only available outside the US) gives 4, 5, 7, 15, 30 or 60 days unlimited travel throughout the USA.

Ferries A ferry service links San Francisco with the Bay communities of Sausalito, Larkspur and Tiburon in scenic Marin County, and to Vallejo, Oakland and Alameda (departures from Pier 1, foot of Market Street). There is also a boat service from Long Beach and Newport Beach to Catalina Island.

Urban Transportation Local communities and major cities are served by local bus services. In addition, San Francisco has cable-cars serving the downtown area and the BART train system covering the Bay areas. Los Angeles has its metrorail and San Diego has a trolley car service through the downtown area.

CAR RENTAL

If planning to rent a car, consider the fly/drive programs many airline offer before you go. Other-wise most car rental companies have offices throughout the state. Charges depend on size of car, locale and time of year. Pay by credit card to avoid hefty cash deposit.

CABS

Cabs may be hailed on the street but few cruise outside tourist areas. If you are away from airports or major hotels it is best to phone for one (look under "cabs" in Yellow Pages). In most cities rates are high, except San Francisco because of its comparatively small size.

DRIVING

Speed limits on rural interstate roads (motorways): **70mph/113kph**

Speed limits on many freeways (two-lane or more carriageways): **65mph/105kph**

Speed limits in residential and business districts and school zones: **25mph/40kph (or as signposted)**

Must be worn in front seats at all times and in rear seats where fitted.

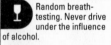

Random breath-testing. Never drive under the influence of alcohol.

Petrol (gasoline or gas), leaded and unleaded, is sold in US gal (3.8L). Most petrol stations are self service. When removing the nozzle from the pump you must lift or turn the lever to activate it. Petrol is more expensive in remote areas and you may be charged more if paying by credit card.

If you break down in a rented car, phone the emergency number on the dashboard. Summon help from emergency telephones located along freeways (every ½ mile) and remote highways (every 2 miles/3km), or sit tight and wait for the cruising highway patrol or state patrol to spot you (a raised bonnet should help).

121

PERSONAL SAFETY

California is certainly not crime free and drugs are a problem, but exercise due caution, especially in downtown areas, and you should be safe. Away from these areas crime is quite low key. Some precautions:

- Do not peer at a map at every street corner, suggesting you are a lost tourist.
- If confronted by a mugger, hand over your money.
- If driving do not stop the car in any unlit or deserted urban area.

Police assistance:

☎ **911**
from any call box

TELEPHONES

Telephones are located in hotel and motel lobbies, drugstores, restaurants, garages and in roadside kiosks. Exact change in 5, 10 and 25 cent pieces is required to place a call. For internal calls dial 1 before the number when the area code is different from the one on the phone you are using. For the operator dial 0, for directory assistance dial 411.

International Dialling Codes

From the USA to:	
UK:	011 44
Germany:	011 49
Netherlands:	011 31
Spain:	011 34

POST

Post Offices
Post offices are plentiful in cities. Stamps are also sold from stamp machines in hotels and shops but have a 25 percent mark up. Main post offices in larger cities normally open 8–6 (noon Sat); closed: Sun. ☎ 213/483 3745 (LA); ☎ 415/487 8981 (San Fran)

ELECTRICITY

The power supply is: 110–115 volts

Round 3-hole sockets taking plugs with 2 flat pins in a parallel position, with an upper, round, earth pin for earthed appliances. European visitors should bring a voltage transformer as well as an adaptor.

TIPS/GRATUITIES

Yes ✓ No ✗		
Restaurants	✓	15–20%
Cafeterias/fast-food outlets	✗	
Bars	✓	15–20%
Cabs	✓	15–20%
Porters	✓	$1/bag
Chambermaids	✓	$1/day
Usherettes	✗	
Hairdressers	✓	10–15%
Cloakroom attendants	✓	$1/coat
Lavatories	✗	

PHOTOGRAPHY

What to photograph: alpine ranges, redwood forests, thundering rivers, crystal-clear lakes, spectacular deserts, sunny beaches, glitzy cities.

Where to buy film: drugstores and supermarkets are probably the cheapest places; you will pay more at specialized kiosks near major tourist attractions.

Video film: the format used for video cassettes in the US differs from that used in the UK. You cannot buy videos in the US compatible with a video camera bought in the UK.

HEALTH

Insurance

There is no agreement for medical treatment between the US and other countries and all travelers MUST be covered by medical insurance (for an unlimited amount of medical costs is advisable). Treatment will be refused without evidence of insurance.

Dental Services

Medical insurance (see above) will cover you for dental treatment. In the event of any emergency, see your hotel concierge or consult the Yellow Pages for an emergency dentist.

Sun Advice

California enjoys a lot of sunshine with more than 250 clear days a year. Along the coast mornings can be hazily overcast and sea breezes (especially in the north) can make it feel cooler than it is. Protect the skin at all times.

Drugs

Quick-remedy medicines such as aspirin are readily available at any pharmacy (drugstore). For tablets containing acetaminophen read paracetamol. Also, many pain-killing pills available "over the counter" at home may need a prescription in the US.

Safe Water

It is quite safe to drink tap water. In hotels and restaurants a nice touch is that water, generally ice cold, is provided free with meals. Bottled water is also widely available but is not as popular as in Europe.

CONCESSIONS

Students Upon production of ID proving student status, there are discounts available on travel, theater and museum tickets, plus at some nightspots. It is always worth asking at the outset.

Senior Citizens For anyone over the age of 62 there is a tremendous variety of discounts on offer (upon proof of age). Both Amtrak (train) and Greyhound (bus), as well as many US airlines, offer (smallish) percentage reductions on fares. Museums, art galleries, attractions, cinemas, and even hotels offer small discounts, and as the definition of senior can drop to as low as 55, it is always worth enquiring.

CLOTHING SIZES

USA	UK	Europe		
36	36	46		Suits
38	38	48		
40	40	50		
42	42	52		
44	44	54		
46	46	56		
8	7	41		Shoes
8.5	7.5	42		
9.5	8.5	43		
10.5	9.5	44		
11.5	10.5	45		
12	11	46		
14.5	14.5	37		Shirts
15	15	38		
15.5	15.5	39/40		
16	16	41		
16.5	16.5	42		
17	17	43		
6	8	34		Dresses
8	10	36		
10	12	38		
12	14	40		
14	16	42		
16	18	44		
6	4.5	38		Shoes
6.5	5	38		
7	5.5	39		
7.5	6	39		
8	6.5	40		
8.5	7	41		

- Contact the airport or airline the day prior to leaving to ensure flight details are unchanged.
- Departure tax: all airport, customs and security taxes are included in the price of the ticket.
- Check the duty-free limits of the country you are entering before departure.

LANGUAGE

English is the official language of the USA. Californians, however, are a fascinating mix of cultures, most notably of Spanish or Mexican extraction. In fact, Spanish is heard throughout California. Spanish is met in many forms, for instance in city and street names. The five largest cities in California: Los Angeles, San Diego, San Francisco, San Jose and Sacramento bear Spanish names. However, although English is the native language there are many differences between its British and American usage. Some of the more commonly encountered are listed below:

holiday	*vacation*	eiderdown	*comforter*
fortnight	*two weeks*	tap	*faucet*
ground floor	*first floor*	luggage	*baggage*
first floor	*second floor*	hotel porter	*bellhop*
second floor	*third floor*	chambermaid	*room maid*
flat	*apartment*	surname	*last name*
lift	*elevator*	cupboard	*closet*

cheque	*check*	25 cent coin	*quarter*
traveller's cheque	*traveler's check*	banknote	*bill*
		banknote (collo-	*greenback*
I cent coin	*penny*	quial)	
5 cent coin	*nickel*	dollar (colloquial)	*buck*
10 cent coin	*dime*	cashpoint	*automatic teller*

aubergine	*eggplant*	biscuit	*cookie*
frankfurter	*frank*	scone	*biscuit*
prawns	*shrimp*	sorbet	*sherbet*
aubergine	*eggplant*	jelly	*jello*
courgette	*zucchini*	jam	*jelly*
maize	*corn*	confectionery	*candy*
chips (potato)	*fries*	spirit	*liquor*
crisps (potato)	*chips*	soft drink	*soda*

car	*automobile*	petrol	*gas, gasoline*
bonnet (of car)	*hood*	railway	*railroad, railway*
boot (of car)	*trunk*	tram	*streetcar*
repair	*fix*	underground	*subway*
caravan	*trailer*	platform	*track*
lorry	*truck*	buffer	*bumper*
motorway	*freeway*	single ticket	*one-way ticket*
main road	*highway*	return ticket	*round-trip ticket*

shop	*store*	policeman	*cop*
chemist (shop)	*drugstore*	post	*mail*
cinema	*movies*	post code	*zip code*
pavement	*sidewalk*	ring up,	*call*
subway	*underpass*	telephone	
gangway	*aisle*	long-distance	*trunk call*
toilet	*lavatory*	call	
trousers	*pants*	autumn	*fall*
nappy	*diaper*	gangway	*aisle*
glasses	*eyeglasses*	pavement	*sidewalk*

INDEX

Acknowledgments
The Automobile Association wishes to thank the following libraries, photographers and associations for their assistance in the preparation of this book.
© DISNEY ENTERPRISES, INC. 18; MARY EVANS 10; RONALD GRANT ARCHIVE 11, 14; ROBERT HARDING 22, ROBERT HOLMES 8a, 31, 44, 62, 63, 64, 67, 87, 88, 89; MRI BANKER'S GUIDE TO FOREIGN CURRENCY 119; PICTURES COLOUR LIBRARY 9b; SPECTRUM COLOUR LIBRARY 27a, 56, 58.
The remaining transparencies are held in the Association's own library (**AA PHOTO LIBRARY**) and were taken by H Harris 15b, 24; R Holmes 2, 6, 7, 8b, 12, 16, 17, 19, 20, 22/3, 25, 26, 35, 36, 38, 39, 40b, 41a, 43, 49, 50, 55, 57, 59, 60, 61, 65, 66, 71a, 71b, 72, 73, 74, 75, 76/7, 81, 82, 83, 84, 85, 86, 90, 91a, 117b, 122a; K Paterson 13, 27b, 33, 34, 37, 40a, 41b, 42, 80a, 91b, 117a, 122b, 122c; B Smith 32; P Wood 1, 5a, 5b, 9a, 15a, 21, 45, 48, 51, 52, 53, 54, 79, 80b.

Author's Acknowledgments
Richard Minnich wishes to thank Mr and Mrs Fred B. Minnich, Ms Karen Hicks, Dr. and Mrs John L. Graves, the Los Angeles branch of the California Film Commission and Mr and Mrs Brian Kaminer for their help with this book.

This book makes reference to various Disney copyrighted characters, trademarks, marks and registered marks owned by The Walt Disney Company and Disney Enterprises, Inc.

Contributors
Revision Management: Apostrophe S Limited   Copy editor: Larry Dunmire   Page layout: Design 23
Verifier: Sheila Hawkins   Researcher (Practical Matters): Colin Follett   Indexer: Marie Lorimer

Dear Essential Traveller

Your comments, opinions and recommendations are very important to us. So please help us to improve our travel guides by taking a few minutes to complete this simple questionnaire.

You do not need a stamp (unless posted outside the UK). If you do not want to cut this page from your guide, then photocopy it or write your answers on a plain sheet of paper.

Send to: **The Editor, AA World Travel Guides, FREEPOST SCE 4598, Basingstoke RG21 4GY.**

Your recommendations...

We always encourage readers' recommendations for restaurants, nightlife or shopping – if your recommendation is used in the next edition of the guide, we will send you a *FREE* **AA *Essential* Guide** of your choice. Please state below the establishment name, location and your reasons for recommending it.

_____

_____

_____

_____

Please send me **AA *Essential*** _____

About this guide...

Which title did you buy?
    AA *Essential* _____
Where did you buy it?_____
When? m̲ m̲ / y̲ y̲

Why did you choose an AA *Essential* Guide? _____

_____

_____

_____

_____

Did this guide meet your expectations?
    Exceeded ☐   Met all ☐   Met most ☐   Fell below ☐
    Please give your reasons_____

_____

_____

_____

continued on next page...

Were there any aspects of this guide that you particularly liked? _____
_____
_____

Is there anything we could have done better? _____
_____
_____

About you...

Name (*Mr/Mrs/Ms*) _____

    Address _____

_____

_____ Postcode _____

    Daytime tel nos _____

Please only give us your mobile phone number if you wish to hear from us about other products and services from the AA and partners by text or mms.

Which age group are you in?
Under 25 ☐   25–34 ☐   35–44 ☐   45–54 ☐   55–64 ☐   65+ ☐

How many trips do you make a year?
Less than one ☐   One ☐   Two ☐   Three or more ☐

Are you an AA member? Yes ☐   No ☐

About your trip...

When did you book? m m / y y   When did you travel? m m / y y
How long did you stay? _____
Was it for business or leisure? _____
Did you buy any other travel guides for your trip?
    If yes, which ones? _____

Thank you for taking the time to complete this questionnaire. Please send it to us as soon as possible, and remember, you do not need a stamp (*unless posted outside the UK*).

Happy Holidays!

The information we hold about you will be used to provide the products and services requested and for identification, account administration, analysis, and fraud/loss prevention purposes. More details about how that information is used is in our privacy statement, which you'll find under the heading "Personal Information" in our terms and conditions and on our website: www.theAA.com. Copies are also available from us by post, by contacting the Data Protection Manager at AA, Fanum House, Basing View, Basingstoke, Hampshire RG21 4EA.

We may want to contact you about other products and services provided by us, or our partners (by mail, telephone) but please tick the box if you DO NOT wish to hear about such products and services from us by mail or telephone. ☐

The Atlas

Acknowledgements
All pictures are from AA World Travel Library with contributions from the following photographers:
Max Jourdan: surfer
Ken Paterson: Broadway district of San Francisco, Oakland Bay Bridge, view of redwoods
Phil Wood: The world famous landmark of the "Hollywood" sign

Day One

Day Two

Day Three

Day Four

EXCHANGES AND REFUNDS

If you are not happy with your purchase, please return it in a saleable condition within 14 days with your receipt for an exchange or refund.
Refunds will be issued to your original payment method.

The Wonder Room, Technology and Furniture Hall have their own policies – please ask in store for details.

This does not affect your statutory rights.

SELFRIDGES&C⁰

EXCHANGES AND REFUNDS

If you are not happy with your purchase,

SELFRIDGES&C°

400 Oxford Street London W1A 1AB
Freephone 0800 123 400
(From overseas + 44 113 369 8040)
V.A.T NO. GB 705 3259 52

You were served by: Rupert Jaques
795   50231409   9780749539443
AA ESSENTIAL CA   *   £5.99

Total 1 Items	£5.99
Cash UK Sterling	£6.00
Change	£0.01

Selfridges have applied VAT at 15% to
the appropriate items in this transaction

Transaction in accordance with
notified terms and conditions

Term 0653 Opr 9999807049 Trans 0081
Store 009999   Date 19/08/09 18:23

0099990653008109081918232329

Day Five

Day Six

Day Seven

www.theAA.com
The Automobile Association's website offers comprehensive and up-to-the-minute information covering AA-approved hotels, guest houses and B&Bs, restaurants and pubs in the UK; airport parking, insurance, European breakdown cover, European motoring advice, a ferry planner, European route planner, overseas fuel prices, a bookshop and much more.

www.aaa.com
AAA's website offers comprehensive information covering AAA-approved hotels and restaurants in the US. In addition, AAA can assist US citizens with obtaining a passport, reservations and tickets for cruise, tour, motorcoach, rail and air travel. AAA provides information on independent or escorted tours for individuals or groups and offers benefits on cruises, tours and travel packages.

The Foreign and Commonwealth Office
Country advice, traveler's tips, before you go information, checklists and more.
www.fco.gov.uk

Visit USA Association
www.visitusa.org.uk

California Division of Tourism
www.visitcalifornia.com

GENERAL
UK Passport Service
www.ukpa.gov.uk

US passport information
www.travel.state.gov

Health Advice for Travelers
www.doh.gov.uk/traveladvice

BBC—Holiday
www.bbc.co.uk/holiday

The Full Universal Currency Converter
www.xe.com/ucc/full.shtml

Flying with Kids
www.flyingwithkids.com

Redwood National and State Parks
www.nps.gov/redw

Yosemite National Park
www.nps.gov/yose

San Francisco Convention and Visitors Bureau
www.sfvisitor.org

www.disneyland.com

TRAVEL
Flights and Information
www.cheapflights.co.uk
www.thisistravel.co.uk
www.ba.com
www.worldairportguide.com

ATLAS SYMBOLS

Highway, multilane divided road - under construction Autobahn, mehrspurige Straße - in Bau		Autoroute, route à plusieurs voies - en construction Autopista, carretera de más carriles - en construcción
Toll road - under construction Gebührenpflichtige Straße - in Bau		Route à péage - en construction Carretera de peaje - en construcción
Trunk road - under construction Fernverkehrsstraße - in Bau		Route à grande circulation - en construction Ruta de larga distancia - en construcción
Principal highway Hauptstraße		Route principale Carretera principal
Secondary road Nebenstraße		Route secondaire Carretera secundaria
Practicable road, track Fahrweg, Piste		Chemin carrossable, piste Camino vecinal, pista
Road numbering Straßennummerierung		Numérotage des routes Numeración de carreteras
Distances in mi. (USA), in km (CDN) Entfernungen in mi. (USA), in km (CDN)		Distances en mi. (USA), en km (CDN) Distancias en mi. (USA), en km (CDN)
Height in meters - Pass Höhe in Meter - Pass		Altitude en mètres - Col Altura en metros - Puerto de montaña
Railway - Railway ferry Eisenbahn - Eisenbahnfähre		Chemin-de-fer - Ferry-boat Ferrocarril - Línea marítima
Major international airport - Airport Wichtiger internationaler Flughafen - Flughafen		Aéroport importante international - Aéroport Aeropuerto importante internacional - Aeropuerto
International boundary - Province boundary Internationale Grenze - Provinzgrenze		Frontièr nationale - Limite ou de província Frontera nacional - Frontera provincial
Time zone boundary Zeitzonengrenze		Limite de fuseau horaire Límite del huso horario
Federal capital Hauptstadt eines Bundesstaates		Capitale d'un état fédéral Capital de estado
Restricted area Sperrgebiet		Zone interdite Zona prohibida
Indian reservation - National park Indianerreservat - Nationalpark		Réserve d'indiens - Parc national Reserva de indios - Parque nacional
Ancient monument Antikes Baudenkmal		Monuments antiques Yacimiento arqueológico
Interesting cultural monument Sehenswertes Kulturdenkmal		Monument culturel intéressant Monumento cultural de interés
Interesting natural monument Sehenswertes Naturdenkmal		Monument naturel intéressant Monumento natural de interés
Well Brunnen		Puits Pozo

Road numbering labels: 1, 48, 1, 26, 26

259 / 130 / 129

Height: 1365

Time zone boundary: -4h Greenwich Time / -3h Greenwich Time

SACRAMENTO

Fort Kent

Niagara Falls

Scale:
0 — 100 km
0 — 50 miles